BUSTLER CLASS RESCUE TUGS

BUSTLER CLASS RESCUE TUGS

IN WAR AND PEACE

R.O. NEISH

Whittles Publishing

Published by
Whittles Publishing Ltd,
Dunbeath,
Caithness, KW6 6EG,
Scotland, UK

www.whittlespublishing.com

© 2022 R.O. Neish

ISBN 978-184995-504-1

CONTENTS

FOREWORD

This is the compelling story of a small but very significant part of work done over many years by His and Her Majesty's Rescue Tugs in defence of the realm, and to the benefit of seafarers all over the world. Ron Neish's very detailed account of the contribution made by HMRT in general, and the Bustler class in particular, is an excellent read, and has brought to life the immense impact that these rescue tugs have had over many years, usually in dire circumstances, most especially during World War II. For instance, in the accounts of the many convoys that crossed the seas and were attacked by hostile forces, who would have thought of mentioning the rescue tugs?

Much has been written about maritime affairs over the centuries and more so during the last century as the means of communication have developed and made reporting so much easier. Photography, and now digital media, have also added hugely to the reporter's ability to record the facts in great detail and present them in graphic form to the benefit of the reader. This account is a fine example of just that, and has raised the profile of these small but immensely powerful and dedicated vessels, and of course their highly skilled crews, without whom these heroic achievements would not have been possible.

As for me, my main link with the Bustler class came in Malta in 1956 when my father, Lieutenant Commander Peter Day, took command of HMS *Mediator*. He had actually joined during the Suez Crisis, during which time *Mediator* was deployed back and forth on many towing missions. After that I was lucky to go to sea in her on a number of occasions, mainly when she was towing targets for cruisers, destroyers, and aircraft to fire upon. Not the most exciting activity for this very able vessel, but more so when the ships managed to cut the tow cable with a shell or severely damage the target, which happened quite frequently. *Mediator*, with her crew of UK and Maltese personnel, some of whom were on national service, was a very happy ship, and was involved in a number of exciting events over the three years, as you will see in Chapter 7. For Dad, who had joined the Royal Navy in 1938 and served in the cruiser *Cumberland* in the South Atlantic and *Cossack* in the North Atlantic before transferring to submarines, *Mediator* was his most enjoyable appointment, and he never stopped talking about her right up until his death in 2007.

I also remember well, as do many others – particularly when enjoying a quiet pint – the now infamous event in 1960 when the battleship HMS *Vanguard* went aground in front of the Still & West pub at the entrance to Portsmouth Harbour, as she set off on her final voyage under tow to the breaker's yard at Faslane in Scotland. I can't remember who was responsible for this slight 'error of judgement' but RFAs *Bustler* and *Samsonia* were in attendance. Along with many others we went down to the Sally Port to see her go. Dad was the last first lieutenant of *Vanguard*, and even though not on board at the time was mortified that she should end up on the putty, albeit in the front garden of that historic pub: 'Wouldn't have happened on my watch,' he said. One can only surmise that the pilot was thirsty and needed a bit of refreshment! Either way, although it was a memorable event, it was not the most elegant departure of that very fine ship of the line.

Finally, not only is this book a great read, but also it should be seen as a valued historical record of the massive contribution made by HMRT, in particular the Bustler class. One cannot admire more the skill and seamanship displayed by all who sailed them over so many years, more often than not in the worst of weather.

Ken Day, Captain Royal Navy (Rtd)

INTRODUCTION

The Admiralty was Henry Robb Shipyard's largest customer, mostly due to the warship building requirements of World War II. As well as warships, the Leith shipyards were called upon to build some much-needed ocean-going rescue tugs. The rescue/salvage tugs did vital work on the North Atlantic convoy route during the Battle of the Atlantic from 1941 to 1944 by helping stricken ships, boosting the war effort by saving hundreds of warships and their crews.

The Royal Navy's Rescue Tug Section had been set up at the beginning of the war to provide suitable ocean-going tugs to help save torpedoed ships. This was dangerous work, requiring the greatest skills to ensure that ships were brought to safe havens despite the often bad weather of the North Atlantic and the presence of enemy submarines and aircraft.

At the start there were only four Royal Navy tugs and eight civilian requisitions available for deep sea work. However, these inadequacies were remedied by concerted action: by the end of the war, due to newly built additions from British and US shipyards, the number of deep sea/salvage tugs had grown to more than 80.

The rescue tugs had a complement of 42 and were manned (at that time women were not sent into active service) by experienced volunteers from the Merchant Navy and the fishing fleets. All were recruited into the Royal Navy under T124 articles, and they formed a specialist unit known as His Majesty's Rescue Tug Service. Many thousands of seamen of all nationalities owe their lives to the brave men who manned the deep sea rescue tugs.

From 1941 the tugs were commanded from HMS Minona in Campbeltown on the Mull of Kintyre in Scotland. Minona had been built in Leith and launched from the Ramage & Ferguson yard in April 1906. As the war progressed, the tugs were also based at Loch Ewe and Oban, and Londonderry in Northern Ireland, and even in Iceland. Later in the war the tugs were based at ports around the Mediterranean. As more tugs became available, they accompanied the slower convoys across the Atlantic and were responsible for towing hundreds of ships to safety after these had been torpedoed or bombed.

From 1943 a rescue tug was attached to every transatlantic convoy. By the end of the war the 'Campbeltown Navy' had helped to save more than 3 million tons of Allied

Fig 1 HMRT *Samsonia,* ex-*Samson*, Ship No 322. Note her for'ard gun. (Image from historical RFA and shown with permission.)

shipping, over 250 warships and hundreds of seamen, mostly in the North Atlantic. Twenty rescue tugs were lost on active service, and in all, 41 deep sea rescue tugs were lost during the war.

Eight of the tugs built in the Leith shipyards of Henry Robb were of the Bustler class. Robb had put a lot of work into this design, and once it had been accepted by the Admiralty full production of the first four went into force. The tugs were ordered in pairs.

These tugs were His Majesty's Rescue Tugs *Bustler, Samsonia, Growler* **and** *Hesperia*, built and launched in 1941/42, all of 1,100 grt. The remaining four rescue tugs, built in 1944/45, were *Mediator, Reward, Turmoil* and *Warden*, all of 1,136 grt.

The Bustler class tugs built by Henry Robb were to serve in battle zones around the oceans; they provided first-class service during the conflict, and some were to go on to feature in rescues worldwide. These long-range rescue tugs were ocean-going ships which often accompanied convoys and operated in all theatres of the war.

They were the first RN fleet tugs powered by two 8-cylinder diesel engines. Their oil fuel capacity was 405 tons, which gave them a range of about 1,700 miles. As completed, the class was armed with one 12-pounder AA gun and one 2-pounder AA gun, plus two 20mm AA and four Lewis .303 machine guns.

The vessels were designed for ocean towing, salvage and rescue, and as they had a 30-ton bollard pull they were too powerful for harbour work. Early in the war they were involved in trials of pressure-minesweeping methods, where a dumb barge was towed behind the tug with the aim of exploding mines intended for merchant ships and warships. Unfortunately, the pressure wave created by the tug alone was sufficient to detonate the mines, so the trials were abandoned.

At the end of the war the class were seen as ideal for commercial charter, and eventually six of them saw service as Royal Fleet Auxiliaries.

On and after D-Day about 160 tugs of all types were deployed in the transportation of the Mulberry harbours across the English Channel to the Normandy beaches. The 59 merchant ships used to form the breakwater were also towed across to be placed. The huge drums containing the Pluto pipeline, which supplied 1.25 million gallons of fuel every day to the Allied armies, were also towed across the Channel by these tugs.

The role of the rescue tugs has been somewhat overlooked, along with the part that they played in the conflict that enveloped the globe to become known as World War II. We have heard much of the roles played out by many other branches of the Royal Navy; this book is but a very small attempt to throw some light on the role played by the rescue tugs, and in particular the role of the eight Bustler class tugs built at Leith.

Admiralty tugs were built to Navy specifications, and standardised where possible to a single design based on a civilian type. They were built by shipyards specialising in tug construction, and thus incorporated merchant features such as an enclosed bridge and wooden superstructure. However, it was specified they be armed, and equipped with radio.

Of all the tugs built during World War II the Bustler class were the most powerful. With a top speed of 16 knots they could get to a rescue quickly, but their speed when towing rescued vessels, even in good weather, was only 5 knots, which meant they were an easy target for any waiting U-boats. It took special ships and special men to carry out this role.

1: THE NEED

The first battle to be fought was not at sea but on land – between the men who knew that they needed ships primarily built for deep sea rescue and salvage work, and the powers that be who had to be convinced of this. As to begin with the Royal Navy had just four of this type of tug, despite Britain having the largest merchant fleet in the world, requests were to go out worldwide to try and secure more tugs. With a war on, however, this was to prove somewhat difficult, to say the least.

The Navy needed new ships and needed the ships quickly, but every other arm of the British military had its own needs as well. Constant badgering of the people in high places was at first met with continual nods of understanding but nothing else: as the war at sea had begun on the day that war had been declared between Britain and Germany, the need for tugs was low on the priority list.

The need for rescue tugs did not rise on the priority list until large numbers of ships started to become casualties of the U-boats. More and more ships and men were being lost to the underwater menace. More and more of Britain's supplies had to come from overseas, but the convoy systems were just beginning to get worked out, and many stragglers from a convoy just had to be left to their fate. With the right type of tug a great many of these ships and men might have been saved.

This extract from the Liverpool War Museum explains the position clearly:

> When the war began the Royal Navy, with the help from Canadian, French and other Allied navies, took on the job of defending British and Allied merchant shipping from German attacks. As in the later stages of the First World War (from 1917–1918), its main means of defence against such attacks was the convoy system. This involved groups of merchant ships sailing in close formation under the protection of one or more escort warships. When the war began, however, Britain and her allies had too few naval escort ships for ocean convoy work. They also had too few long-range aircraft available to provide adequate air cover for Atlantic convoys.

The convoys

From the first day of the war, the Admiralty organized most British and Allied ships crossing the Atlantic into convoys. These originally consisted of up to 30 or 40 merchant ships sailing in lines or columns under the protection of one or more naval escort ships. In later war years, Atlantic convoys became much larger, often exceeding 70 ships.

Convoys were the basis of an 'interlocking system of shipping traffic'. This meant that ocean convoys were distributed into coastal convoys for passage to and from UK East Coast and West Country ports. Coastal shipping around less vulnerable parts of the British coast did not usually sail in convoy.

At the outbreak of war, the Royal Navy was desperately short of ships suitable for convoy escort work. It had available for convoy duties less than 24 old destroyers, a handful of sloops and a few anti-submarine trawlers. In the winter of 1940, there were not enough escorts to provide two for each convoy and the Admiralty had to call on the services of 70 trawlers from the fishing fleets. They also had too few long-range aircraft available to provide adequate air cover for Atlantic convoys. This left a fatal 'Air Gap' in mid-Atlantic which the U-boats were to exploit with devastating effect during the early war years.

From August 1941 the need to protect the vital convoys to North Russia caused a further drain on the Royal Navy's resources. This was partly balanced by the growing role of the Royal Canadian Navy in the North Atlantic.

In September 1940, 50 old US destroyers were transferred to the Royal Navy in return for the gift or lease to the USA of British naval and air bases in the western Atlantic islands. These old but sturdy ships were to do vital work in escorting Atlantic convoys.

Until July 1941 Atlantic convoys leaving or approaching Britain only had naval escorts within 150 miles west or south of Ireland. For almost the first two years of war ships were usually unescorted for the greater part of the Atlantic crossing.

Towards the end of 1939 incoming Atlantic convoys were singled out for attack by German U-boats. The most critical time was after the division of a convoy west of Ireland, when small groups of ships would sale for port with only one destroyer to each group. The 8,000 ton 'Malabar' was torpedoed by the German submarine U-34 some 50 miles west of the Scilly Isles in the early hours of 29th October 1939. She sank the following afternoon. 'Malabar' had left convoy HX5 (Halifax, Nova Scotia, to Britain) to take the southern route around Ireland in the company of an oil tanker and the destroyer 'HMS Grafton'. She had been bound for London and Avonmouth with tobacco, lumber and general cargo. Five out of her crew of eighty-one were lost.

Fig 2 *Bustler* (photo from Historicalrfa.com).

There was an obvious need to augment the fleet of ocean-going tugs, and a call went out to the shipyards of the United Kingdom to see if a solution to this dire situation could be provided – and provided fast.

Experience learned from World War I and through the 1920s and 1930s dictated that the Admiralty should use a proven design that could be built in a commercial shipyard, and the answer was to be provided by the Leith shipyards of Henry Robb. After much back and forth by the Admiralty with regard to the eventual design of the class, *Bustler* was to be the first in line of a total of eight built at the shipyard.

This was to all change rapidly, however, when Holland and the rest of the Low Countries fell to the German onslaught. Hard on the heels of the retreat from Dunkirk and the fall of France, the Germans were quick to take over as many vessels as they could, putting guns on them and using them as convoy rescue tugs for themselves.

The Admiralty now faced a crisis. They could not take the few ocean-going tugs that they had on station covering the eastern seaboard of the United States; those vessels were too valuable to be used for convoy duty. So the only solution was to build, and to build more; but every other part of the forces also required more – more guns, more aircraft and so on.

There was also the time it would take to design such craft; what was required was a large seagoing vessel capable of rescue and towing large ships over many miles of ocean. There was an initial rough design at the Admiralty, a sound design that would require preliminary lines and scantlings before it could be taken to a shipyard.

The ship had to be over 1,000 tons, diesel-engined with twin screws, fitted for towing and salvage work and with a cruising range of 15,000 miles – a tall order for any shipyard to take on.

Never mind that all the yards in Britain were flat out, building merchantmen or warships to try and replace the losses now being incurred regularly with the U-boats having almost free range over the North Atlantic routes.

Once the preliminary plans were ready it was Henry Robb of Leith that the Admiralty approached, as this yard was well known for building fine, stout ships. Asked how long it would take, they replied, 'Around nine months to one year.'

'Too long,' came the laconic reply from the Admiralty.

'With the right backing we could perhaps do it in three months,' said the shipyard.

'You will have all the backing you require,' replied the Admiralty.

So it was that the shipyard of Henry Robb was entrusted with the build and final design of eight ships that would form the Bustler class.

They would have twin diesel engines but only one propeller, the two engines providing the power to a single shaft.

The preliminary lines would be taken by the mould loft, and the laying off and fairing would commence almost immediately. Only once the lines had been faired could a complete and finished offset book be supplied to the drawing office, which could then begin producing the many steelwork drawings that would be used, along with the hundreds of templates made in the mould loft.

The men could then go about the business of building the ship, with her keel laid down first, and then her frames would be erected and horned into place by the shipwrights. Once in frame she would be ready to take her shell, and week by week she would grow and assume the more familiar shape of a completed ship.

Despite all the assurances and the desperate need for these ships, the Admiralty could not keep from interfering – as is so often the way with officialdom – with the design and build of the ships, and this interference created a great many delays. The Admiralty, with their prolonged meetings, stalling the build in discussions about comparatively minor points of equipment – points which could have been discussed and sorted out while the

Fig 3 HMS *Mediator* sailing from Malta, December 1956. (I was sent this image by Capt Ken Day, with his permission to use it.)

build was continuing – continued to present frustration to the shipbuilder, and as it turned out these delays took up months, with the first build eventually taking more than a year.

All the while convoys were going out to battle the elements and the U-boats with only one tug in attendance; sometimes the attending tug would even have to turn around in mid-Atlantic to join a convoy going in the opposite direction.

Some merchant ships were fitted with improvised towing gear, and some armed trawlers were allocated to rescue/salvage work; they tried their best to do a job that they were just not fitted for.

All the while the perfect rescue tug lay on the stocks at the Leith shipyard. Instead of the three months envisaged by the builders it was almost 18 months before HMS *Bustler* would be ready for sea.

2: THE SHIPYARD

Leith had a shipbuilding pedigree that stretched back over 550 years with a DNA in building ships that stretched back to the 14th century.

At the start of World War II, the shipyard that formed the Henry Robb Shipbuilders & Engineering Co. Ltd was an amalgamation of the three former yards that had occupied the site for many years previous. They occupied a site on the edges of the sprawling Leith Docks complex, docks that ranged from Seafield in the east to bordering on Newhaven in the west. There was a total of nine slipways to build ships on.

Until 1924 Henry Robb had operated around the fringes of the docks, wherever he and his firm could find suitable land or dry docks to build in. The first ship that they built, in the early 1920s, was a small tug named *Westmere*; it was built mostly as sub-assemblies and riveted together in a dry dock leased from the Leith Dock Commission, as the young company had no access to the sea.

When the old-established company of Hawthorns & Co closed down, Robb took the site over and now had access to a proper shipyard. With the acquisition of the three building berths that had been Hawthorns, Henry Robb now had direct access to building and launching ships directly into the Firth of Forth for launching ships. Hawthorns had built tugs particularly during World War I for the Admiralty, so it was only natural that the Henry Robb yard would continue in the building of such specialised vessels. In addition, there was no need for drag chains when launching ships from the Victoria Shipyard, as it was now called, as they had a great expanse of sea to launch the vessels into.

A couple of years later another of the older shipyards, Cran & Somerville, also closed down, and Henry Robb took that site over as well. With the takeover of that yard, the firm of Henry Robb now had another ready workforce that specialised in building tugs. So it was no great surprise that his firm would go on to build a great many tugs, along with many other special ships.

In the next decade Robb took over the yards of the well-known builders, Ramage & Ferguson, now closed down.

Fig 4 *Saturno* was ordered in August 1927. (This photograph is taken from an old bound collection given me by the grandson of a former foreman loftsman at the Henry Robb Shipyard. William Wallace was his name, and he was happy to be able to show me some more of the great photographs from the collection, which would appear to have been made to celebrate the building and launch of this fine salvage vessel.)

Fig 5 *Saturno* almost ready to launch (another photograph from the collection).

Fig 6 *Saturno* on her sea trials in the Firth of Forth, before handover and delivery to her owners. She would then head out over the Atlantic to take up station in South America. (Another image from the collection.)

So with nine building berths Henry Robb was well positioned for the many orders that would come in from the Admiralty as Britain declared war with Germany on 3 September 1939.

The first ocean-going salvage tug to be built at the yard was destined for work in Brazil; she was for her day a large and powerful tug. Ship No 81, *Saturno*, was launched in May 1928. She was described as a twin-screw salvage tug of 203 grt.

Saturno would be followed by the larger tug *Pharos* in the following year; she was an order for work in Egypt. *Pharos* was launched in May 1929; this twin-screw salvage tug, at 303 grt, was Ship No 134 in the shipyard order book. The need for larger and faster salvage/towing tugs reflected the larger sizes that ships had now grown to; and with the seas becoming ever more crowded the requirement for tugs that could go to the rescue at a moment's notice was well recognised – the faster they could get to a casualty the better chance of salvage, hence the much larger salvage monies to be won.

S. Paulo, another twin-screw salvage tug at 263 grt, would follow in April 1930, and with the large twin-screw salvage tug *Cochin* going to India in 1933 the yard was also building smaller harbour tugs in between times.

In 1936 they built their largest salvage tug to date, *Abeille No 8*, at 126.7 feet × 33.9 × 13.2. She was a single-screw vessel at 402 grt, powered by a triple-expansion steam engine with three cylinders producing 1265 ihp, built by Aitchison Blair.

Abeille No 8, Ship No 226, an order from the famous French towing company Comp. de Remorquage et Sauvetage, was built to help the two new Cunard Queens manoeuvre in the port of Le Havre before they would take off on their transatlantic voyages.

Abeille No 8 had been built and launched in 1936, only three years before the outbreak of World War II, and unsurprisingly, once the port had been overrun by the Germans advancing into France in 1940 this modern and powerful tug was taken as a prize by them and used in the war against the British. But then, two years to the day after she had been commissioned into the German navy, she was sunk by Allied war planes, who bombed the port and the shipping in it.

Fig 7 *Abeille No 8* on the right of this picture, with *Abeille No 22*, towing a floating dock in 1939. (Copyright unknown; from an image sent to me many years ago from Germany.)

Fig 8 *Saturno* was still in operation at the beginning of this century, and was seen working in 2006. She was last seen shortly afterwards, laid up in a creek in Brazil, and by the time of writing has most likely been scrapped. (Another image from the collection I was given.)

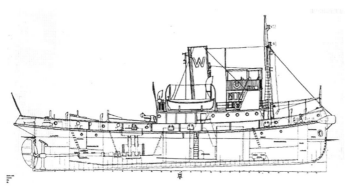

From the time of the launch of *Abeille No 8* to the start of World War II Henry Robb also won orders to build tugs for the Manchester Ship Canal Company – tugs that would be very welcome as the war progressed, able to take larger ships along the canal right into the heart of the industrial powerhouse that Manchester had become.

Outside wartime tugs usually had a long and useful working life, many lasting for upwards of 50 to 60 years, with some going on even longer.

The illustrations above show the progression in the size and design of the large ocean-going salvage tugs built from 1928 with *Saturno* to 1933 and *Cochin*.

With a well-known record for building tugs it was no great surprise to Robb's shipyard to be approached to help design and then build what would become the Bustler class tugs, and as it so happened they were already well down the road with just such a design.

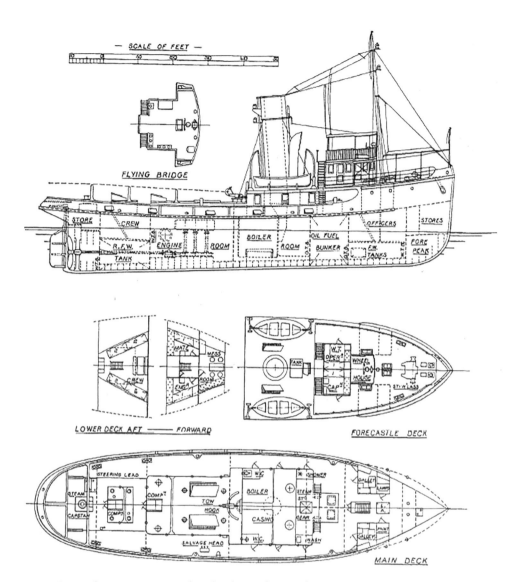

Fig 9 General arrangement and scale plans of *S. Paulo* (general arrangement is from my own collection).

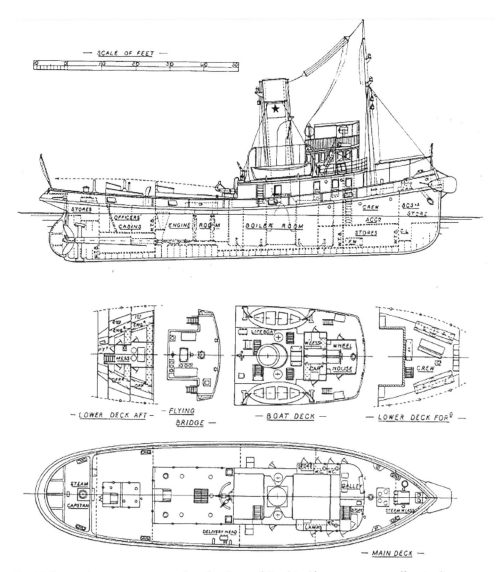

Fig 10 General arrangement and scale plans of *Cochin* (from my own collection).

3: THE CONTEXT

The following are the three main historical events that involved the eight Bustler class tugs built from 1941 to 1945 at the Leith Shipyard of Henry Robb Ltd.

BACKGROUND – THE BATTLE OF THE ATLANTIC

While there have been many books written on the Battle of the Atlantic it may help you to learn a bit about the background to the great need for these special ships.

The following is taken from the book *The Tattie Lads* by Ian Dear, on the role of the men sailing on the rescue tugs during both world wars:

> We conformed, when necessary, in order to placate the Admiralty, otherwise we went our own way, quietly proud of the job we did, which, by its very nature, was often carried out in the worst of conditions and in the knowledge that we were frequently somebody's last hope.

Their attitude was well expressed by one of their officers, Jack Close, who later remarked in his memoir, *Beyond the Horizon*: 'A dislike of authority and a grudging adherence to law and order characterized the service, the officers being no exception.'

The Battle of the Atlantic, which lasted from 2 September 1939 until the defeat of Germany in May 1945, was the war's longest continuous military campaign. It was a fight for Britain's very survival. Winston Churchill, Great Britain's wartime prime minister, asserted that the 'U-boat peril' was the only thing that ever really frightened him during World War II.

The first Atlantic convoy sailed on 2 September 1939, the day before Britain declared war on Germany. The convoys started out with 15–30 ships, and later they were formed into several columns of ships with up to five ships in each column, forming a big box. By the middle of May 1943 the convoys would consist of up to 60–70 ships.

During the six years of naval warfare, German U-boats and warships – and, later, Italian submarines – were pitted against the Allied convoys transporting military equipment and supplies across the Atlantic to Great Britain and Russia.

The Atlantic covers over 100 million square kilometres. This battle to control the Atlantic shipping lanes involved thousands of ships and stretched across thousands of perilous miles of ocean.

As an island, Britain was very much dependent on the supply of raw materials, even in peacetime. This situation was aggravated by the country now fighting for its very survival. Goods had to be delivered by sea, with the country requiring more than a million tons of material and goods every week. Without these supplies the British would not be able to continue taking the fight to the Germans and their Axis allies.

The Germans were aware that Britain's survival depended on the supply of all kinds of goods from overseas. If they could stifle this supply, then Britain would effectively be out of the fight and Germany could concentrate all its military might against the Russians in the east.

While the convoy system allowed vast amounts of goods to get through there was an extremely high price to pay, both in ships and men. While more rescue ships were at last being converted, the rescue/salvage tugs were desperately needed to follow the convoys, picking up survivors where they could and trying to tow stricken ships to the nearest safe haven.

As 1942 moved on, American manufacturing might was getting itself sorted out, and massive amounts of men and material were shipped over the Atlantic as the Allies now began to hit back. Thoughts were turning to the invasion of Europe to wrest back the countries from the Germans and ultimately defeat Germany and her allies.

The Battle of the Atlantic would be fought over millions of square miles of ocean, involving thousands of ships and men, as both sides would claim the upper hand. As the battles moved to and fro across the unpredictable Atlantic Ocean, weapons, tactics and equipment were constantly being developed to try and gain an advantage. This was turning into a war which would be won by the side that could produce the most ships and men; as the U-boats sank shipping faster than the ships could be built, this was an extremely dangerous time in the history of the British nation.

The German must have forgotten the lessons of history, as they had waged a U-boat campaign during World War I, and in 1917 they had had come awfully close to defeating Britain. But in spite of this experience Germany apparently underestimated the impact of U-boats, fighting with only 46 operational vessels and using mostly surface vessels such as their mighty new battlecruisers (which were in fact battleships operating under a different description to by-pass the treaties that had been set up to prevent them building such vessels.) They favoured the large surface ships rather than submarines to hunt for victims amongst the sea lanes of the Atlantic Ocean. This, however, had a limited success rate, leading to the loss of some of Germany's prized capital warships, including the *Graf Spee* and the mighty *Bismarck*.

Nevertheless the control of the seas was still seen through the eyes of the admirals who wanted large capital ships to project power. The German U-boats were yet to be used to their full destructive capabilities, due to squabbles within the German High Command. Although it had turned out that a battleship could be destroyed by air attack or by torpedo, at that stage of the war the Germans apparently never realised that they had a potential war-winning weapon in the U-boat.

On 3 September 1939, the day Britain declared war on Germany after the Germans had invaded Poland under false pretences of protecting their own borders, the British liner *Athenia* was torpedoed by a U-boat. This cowardly and horrible act marked the beginning of the Battle of the Atlantic.

In 1939 the then First Lord of the Admiralty, Winston Churchill, was credited with the reintroduction of the convoy system. Britain managed to survive the early part of the war due to several factors, including the development of improved tactics. Flower class corvettes were quickly built, but in small numbers that made only a little difference at first. These warships, less than 1,000 tons, were based on an early whalecatcher design originally produced by Smith's Dock of Middlesbrough, and they helped plug the gaps in the Royal Navy's escort capability. Many of the Flower class corvettes were built at the Leith shipyards of Henry Robb Ltd. (You will be able to read much more about them in my next book, *Leith Shipyards at War*)

At the start of the war the U-boats were mostly deployed not too far from home on the coasts of northern Germany, so until the fall of France their range in the vast reaches of the Atlantic Ocean was somewhat limited. But with the building of huge U-boat pens on the Atlantic coast of France, this range restriction would soon change, and there would be many innovations in submarine building, as well. So from 1940 onwards the German navy began to focus much more attention on escalating the U-boat war in the open ocean.

The U-boats had great success against the convoys; they would sneak up on one at night underwater then attack on the surface, undetected by sonar or ASDIC, before swiftly submerging once more to evade the searches by the escorting warships. With the aid of decoded messages from the British Admiralty, this tactic added to the potent force that the U-boats were fast becoming: in 1941 alone they accounted for the sinking of 875 Allied ships.

The desperate need for ships to protect the convoys during 1941 was helped to a certain extent by a tremendous effort by Canadian shipbuilders to get the industry organised and start producing Flower class corvettes there as well, as escort vessels. This, with the addition of 50 old destroyers from the US Navy in exchange for American access to British bases, in the Lend Lease Agreement, meant that the convoys would at least have a bit more protection on the dangerous trip over the Atlantic and back.

RAF Coastal Command could help to provide some air cover over part of the route, but range restrictions dictated, and lack of suitable aircraft limited the cover they could provide.

This was also the year that Britain managed to get hold of one of the Enigma machines from the captured U-110, along with the codes which enabled Bletchley Park to decipher the German messages.

From April that year, the US Navy, although still technically neutral, began escorting the slow-moving convoys go as far as Iceland, before breaking away. This was to lead to many clashes between US ships and the U-boats as by this time the U-boats did not regard any non-Axis ship as neutral.

In October 1941 U-562 attacked and sank the US escort ship *Reuben James*, but still the USA, swayed by the huge number of German sympathisers in America, stayed out of the war.

Meanwhile, the Royal Canadian Navy, which had been tiny in 1939, began an amazing period of growth that would eventually made it capable of taking on a substantial part of the fighting in the North Atlantic.

The convoys were still very vulnerable in what was known as the Atlantic Gap – a huge area of sea that was not covered by anti-submarine aircraft; this vulnerability was to lead to the much-improved anti-submarine techniques now quickly being developed. So Britain was now also building what was known as improvised aircraft carriers (escort carriers); the builders, such as Burntisland Shipbuilders in Fife, Scotland, would take the hull of a standard cargo vessel of around 8,000 to 10,000 tons and equip it with a landing deck and air-control bridge. All this led to a marked decrease in the number of losses caused by U-boats towards the end of this year – losses that contributed to the decision by Adolf Hitler (much against his Admiral Dönitz's wishes) to move many of the U-boats to the Mediterranean.

But then, as the combatants moved into 1942, the balance of the Battle of the Atlantic would swing once more in the Germans' favour. This was achieved by a rapid escalation of submarine building by the Axis forces, who were launching 20 U-boats per month. So between January 1942 and June, the convoy losses were growing once more, with over 500 ships sunk; this despite the entry of the Americans into the war. This was to be the year when the battle was almost lost – Allied ship sinkings reached a peak of 1,664. With supplies of petrol and food dropping to critical levels in Great Britain, never was there a greater need for more ships, and more rescue ships for the survivors.

By early 1943 Dönitz, now Commander of the German Navy, had 200 operational U-boats which could be unleashed into the Atlantic to work together in small fleets; these quickly became known as wolf packs.

Britain's supplies of oil were running out, so there was now a battle between shipyards as to how fast they could build the ships to replace the huge losses out at sea. Not just ships, of course; there was also the human suffering and misery of mariners fighting for survival in the frigid waters of an unforgiving ocean.

American manufacturing was swinging into full production, and the mass production of simple cargo ships, to be known as Liberty ships, would help plug the gap in the losses

Fig 11 An Allied convoy crossing the Atlantic during World War II (photo, US Navy).

of ships, although the great loss of life could never be replaced. And then by the middle of 1943, the tide had well and truly turned, with the U-boat losses at record levels. This could not be sustained by a nation now fighting on two fronts, and Dönitz called off the U-boat war as it stood. Germany had lost 45 submarines during April and May, while this was by no means the end of the U-boats in the Atlantic the threat had diminished somewhat.

Although new German submarines, Types XXI and XXIII, arrived in 1944/5, they came far too late to affect the course of the Battle of the Atlantic. German submarine technology was far ahead of anything that the Allies had produced, and if those new types had been introduced earlier they would have presented a serious threat once more to the supply of food, men and materials needed to fight and eventually win the war.

TO SUM UP THE BATTLE OF THE ATLANTIC

You could say that Germany's best hope of defeating Britain lay in winning the Battle of the Atlantic. If Germany had been able to prevent merchant ships from carrying food, raw materials, and troops and their equipment from North America to Britain, the outcome of World War II could have been radically different. Britain, with her armies unable to continue without the required fuel and war material, which all had to be shipped over the Atlantic, could have been starved into suing for peace on German terms. Without control of the seas, it would have been almost impossible to land the Allied forces in North Africa and mainland Europe, and we could now be living in a completely different world.

The Battle of the Atlantic was the longest campaign of World War II, and it was proportionally among the costliest. Estimates say that between 75,000 and 85,000 Allied sailors were killed. Historians estimate that more than 100 convoy battles took place during the war. They cost the Merchant Navy around 3,000 ships and more than 30,000 people. The losses to the Germans amounted to 783 U-boats, with around 28,000 sailors, some two-thirds of those perishing during the Battle of the Atlantic.

Into this madness of human misery entered the rescue/salvage vessels which were to play their part in this momentous time in history.

BACKGROUND: OPERATION PLUTO

It is an old saying that an army marches on its stomach, meaning that for the army to have any chance of success its soldiers require a steady supply of food.

In 1944, mechanised armies required not just food but fuel. This was the huge problem and the huge challenge facing the planners of the upcoming invasion of France and the rest of Europe. Just how to supply enough fuel would occupy the minds of the experts in oil and logistics for most of late 1943 and early 1944. It was not, of course, only for the D-Day invasion that some type of supply line would be needed, but for the continuance of the army's movements. This was a requirement that had been thought about long before any planning had begun for the invasion of France. Initial talks on the challenge had taken place in early 1942 between government officials and some of the leaders of the giant oil companies.

At first two types of pipe were developed, the first one was flexible with a 3-inch diameter lead core. This was a heavy pipe, based on an idea from Siemens Brothers working in conjunction with the National Physics Laboratory, taken from existing undersea telegraph cables. This was just a start, however, as the developers and the army soon realised that the amount of lead required to produce the pipe was not available, and even if it had been the cost would have been prohibitive.

So it was decided that some alternative would have to be found – one that was cheaper, and faster to manufacture and deliver. So they turned their attention to pipe made from mild steel, a plentiful material, and much cheaper.

It was decided that they would nevertheless go ahead with the lead pipe, known as HAIS (the initials of the people credited with coming up with the idea), but also that further investigation into the cheaper form of pipe was to go ahead simultaneously. The engineers involved quickly got to work and came up with a second type. This steel pipe, developed by engineers from the Iraq Petroleum Company and Burmah Oil Company, was less flexible. It would be known as HAMEL, after the two principal engineers involved in its development. During initial testing of the Hamel pipe, it was discovered that due to its lower flexibility it would be best used for most of the pipeline's length, with the Hais type for the sections at each end.

The next challenge to be faced would be the one involved in laying the new steel pipe; its relative inflexibility meant they would need to invent a new way of delivering it. This was solved by a new apparatus based on the principle of a cotton thread wound around a wooden reel, only on a much larger scale. The steel pipe, while rather rigid, could still be wound around a large-diameter drum and then unwound as the drum was towed forward on the surface of the sea. The device was quickly christened the Conundrum, hopefully confusing the enemy should they hear about it.

Once the first of the prototypes was ready, in May 1942, they set out to test it; a shallow-water test was conducted in the Medway, and a deep-water test in the Clyde. Then in June 1942 the Post Office cable ship *Iris* laid lengths of Hais and Hamel pipes in the Clyde. The idea was now formally incorporated into the plans for the invasion of Europe. Many trials and tests were still to be carried out, and ships that could lay the Hais pipes had to be sourced. The existing cable ships were not large enough and did not have the loading or laying equipment that could carry this out successfully. So the War Office set about finding ships that could be converted to cope with the laying of the pipe. Several merchant ships were converted to pipe-laying vessels by stripping out the interiors and fitting them with large cylindrical steel drums, then fitting special hauling gear and suitable sheaves and guides. The Petroleum Warfare Department contracted the firm of Johnson & Phillips for the special gear required to handle and lay the pipe.

The steel pipe, however, could not be bent to a radius of less than 5 feet, so a new drum would have to be manufactured with a 10-foot diameter and fleeting ring. The ships would also require a roller-type bow and stern gear. This final equipment was fitted to yet another Leith-built ship, HMS *Holdfast* (she had been SS *London* when first launched by the Leith Shipyard of Hawthorns & Co. in 1921 as Ship No 183.).

With testing completed with reasonable results, it was time for any spare production capacity to be used, and companies all over Britain were involved in this massive undertaking. Due to lack of manufacturing capacity for the heavy lead-based Hais pipeline, some of this was carried out in America. The codename given to the pipeline system was PLUTO (PipeLine Underwater Transportation of Oil).

The initial production runs of 2-inch pipe were found to be unable to supply enough fuel over the required distance, so the pipe size was increased to 3 inches. This proving a success, it was put into production and the pipes were wound onto the huge drums fitted inside the newly converted ships, HMS *Holdfast* being joined by two more converted vessels, HMS *Sandcroft* and HMS *Latimer*. Each of the ships could handle approximately 100 miles of the pipe, weighing around 6,000 tons.

Many experiments were carried out, mostly in the Bristol Channel, both to prove that the pipe could work and also to help train the many servicemen who would be required to operate the equipment for use in the invasion of Europe,

The Allies knew that it would probably be some time before they could capture a main deep-water port such as Antwerp, and then there would be the time needed to get the port back into operation; the Germans had most of the ports filled with blockships standing by ready to be sunk, and as the Allies got closer the Germans would destroy what they could, to prevent the Allies using the ports. So if the Allies were to invade Europe and push on from any stronghold on the beaches, they would have to ensure a reliable supply of fuel for their tanks and trucks. A single Sherman M4 tank required 150 US gallons to drive 100 miles, and the Allies ultimately landed these tanks in the thousands, along with hundreds of thousands of other mechanised vehicles, so the need for fuel was massive.

Following successful trials of full-size prototypes in early 1944, six of the Conundrums were fabricated to a modified design at Scunthorpe and erected in Tilbury docks, then launched into the Thames. Each of them had a diameter of 30 feet, weighed around 250 tons empty, and had a capacity of up to 60 nautical miles of Hamel pipe.

It was hoped that with the use of both systems enough fuel would reach the frontline troops; but the pipes had to laid on the seabed in a single continuous quick procedure – no mean feat, as the vessels would be steaming slowly and so would be a prime target for

Fig 12 A Sherman tank of 13th/18th Royal Hussars in action against German troops using a crashed Horsa glider as cover near Ranville, 10 June 1944 (photo, Imperial War Museum).

enemy submarines and the fast E-boats. The vessels might also come within range of some of the coastal batteries set up all along the French coast.

The Hais pipe would be taken by the cable-laying ships, the pipe unwinding as they moved forward across the Channel, while the steel Hamel pipe would be unwound from the Conundrums towed by tugs. The Bustler class were the ideal tugs for the job, as they were the most powerful tugs available.

The first line to France was laid on 12 August over a course of more than 100 miles, from Shanklin in the Isle of Wight to Cherbourg.

This failed, however, when a passing ship – some reports say a US escorting destroyer – caught the pipeline with her anchor; other reports laid the cause at the door of a passing troopship. Repairs to undersea cables were, however, still a problem as technology was a little bit behind the practical when it came to being able to conclude repairs with any great success. Attaching the ends of the pipes was also a relatively new procedure and would cause many problems with failures along the way. Even so, the first practical pipeline came into operation in September 1944, some three months late. A total of 21 pipelines, including 6 Hamels, were laid as the fighting moved closer to the German border.

During the great secrecy surrounding the Allies' plans for D-Day many of the pumping stations on the south coast of England were housed in inconspicuous buildings, including ones disguised as cottages and garages. Some of these are still around today, one of them operating as a bed & breakfast accommodation.

The pipeline across the Channel was linked from a large network of fuel lines stretching across England, all the way from ports such as Liverpool and Bristol: all in all, around

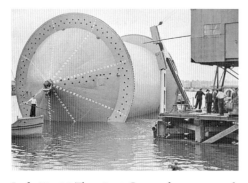 

Left: **Fig 13** The giant Conundrum wound with the Hamel steel pipe used for Operation Pluto. As it is towed it lays the fuel line. (A still from a Universal Studios Newsreel, *Victory Pipeline*, 4 June 1945.)

Right: **Fig 14** A Conundrum, with a total weight of some 1,600 tons, being towed by two tugs, one of them tethered at the rear to help with the steering of the steel pipe, which was difficult to lay. Moreover, the experts had predicted that the pipe would have a working life of only around six weeks. (Image from Imperial War Museum via Wikipedia.)

900 miles of pipework. Once the line was connected on the far shore this pipeline would be extended across the French countryside as the troops moved forward, to end at the Rhine.

Although Operation Pluto received much publicity after the war it was in the event only partially successful. It is recorded, for example, that the battle for Normandy was won without any of the fuel used in it being delivered by Pluto, and eventually only 8 per cent of the fuel delivered to the Allied forces in north-west Europe over the year between D-Day and VE Day came through the pipeline. Most of the fuel was instead delivered by tankers or small coasters full of cased petrol, and some was delivered by air once the French airfields had been secured.

What was successful and can be in no doubt was the huge engineering effort made to produce this complex pipeline system under wartime restrictions and conditions. The pipelines were the forerunners of the flexible pipes used in the development of Britain's offshore oilfields after the war.

After the war more than 90 per cent of the sunken pipe was recovered, as the lead-filled pipe was valuable. An extensive salvage operation was carried out from September 1946 to October 1949. HMS *Holdfast*, by then renamed *Empire Taw*, was involved in the salvage, and it turned out that the value of the scrap raised far outweighed the cost of the operation.

BACKGROUND: THE SUEZ CRISIS

With the nationalisation of the Suez Canal by the Egyptian Leader Gamal Abdel Nasser in July 1956, tensions had reached boiling point between Britain, already under pressure to give up its claims to the region known as the Canal Zone, created by treaty in 1936. Britain and France joined together to put a plan in place to invade the zone and take back the canal.

All the while Egypt was also engaged in sporadic fighting with Israel in the border areas between the two countries. Nasser, as he was commonly referred to in the West, was no lover of Israel or of the country's attempts to enlarge the area it had settled to create the new Zionist nation.

The Egyptians, well supported by money and arms from the Soviet Union, were angry with the United States for reneging on its promise to provide backing and funds for the construction of the Aswan Dam, which was planned to provide power to the country. Nasser took it upon himself to issue orders that the canal should be seized and then nationalised, asserting that the tolls raised from the shipping passing through this very busy waterway could provide the funds required for the building of the dam.

The then British prime minister, Anthony Eden, worked secretly to gain the support of the French and the Israeli forces to retake the canal by means of an armed assault. This was only three years after the end of the war in Korea, and as Britain was still dealing with communist insurgencies in Malaya and Indonesia, it had a very capable army, backed by a modern navy and air force.

The first strike in Egypt was carried out by the Israelis, who needed no excuse to attack their neighbours. The three countries had planned to strike simultaneously, but delays meant that this strike was followed two days later by the assault from British and French forces, the British primarily landing at Port Said and the French at Port Fuad. Although they were behind schedule, they ultimately took over the area, bringing the canal back under their control.

But the delay by the British and French forces had given the Soviet Union an opening. They were putting down an insurrection in Hungary at the time and were keen to exploit any avenue they could to divert world attention from this; the Arab nationalism struggle presented them with just such an opportunity.

No strangers to the Middle East, the Soviets had been supplying Nasser with arms made in Czechoslovakia and they would also help Egypt with the construction of the mighty Aswan Dam. The Soviet leader, Nakita Khrushchev, raged against the invasion, even threatening to send nuclear missiles into the skies of Western Europe if the invading forces did not withdraw. As mentioned previously all this was just three years or so after the Korean War, a war that was not officially over, as the two sides had only signed an armistice agreement.

It was into this time of conflict in a very unstable world that HMS *Warden* was called to provide towing for some of the landing craft from Cyprus to Port Said. The following is a story from Tony Gathercole, on one of the landing craft at the time.

HMS *WARDEN* – Landings Port Said – Gulf Crisis 1950s

All the crew, 11 of us, were men who had completed national service and were recalled as reservists, On the 2/3rd of November I was told to go with crew to Limassol, a Z craft had just completed having its refit there, we were to make ready for the Bustler class tug that would be arriving to tow us over to Egypt.

When *Warden* arrived, we were not quite ready, a little work was still to be done with the ramp, also both engines were playing up (she was twin screw) it was something to do with fuel supply. The skipper of *Warden* wanted to sail, as soon as possible, he had orders to take another Z craft from Famagusta with us to Egypt. It was just after midday, and he would have liked to be underway. It was decided, after a delay of an hour or two, we would go. One engine had been sorted; the other engine the craft engineer would deal with on the way over.

I remember the skipper of *Warden* saying to me if I get any problems on the way, let him know on the radio, he was surprised when I told him I did not have a radio on board. Top marks to him; he gave me a box containing a handheld Aldis lamp. (Fortunately, there was no call to use it.) We soon arrived in Famagusta for the other Z craft, this was taken in tow.

At last we got underway and the towing hawser was played out until we were about quarter of a mile astern of *Warden*. The other Z craft about the same distance astern of us, the weather was reasonable. After dark the weather worsened, the Z craft was a flat bottom vessel, and wasn't the best craft to be aboard at sea in bad weather. *Warden* increased our speed during the night, we must have been moving at 10+knots, no trouble for *Warden* with her 3000+ H.P.

Sleep was not coming easy that night. All the accommodation aboard was aft, by the engine room. With the sea hitting the bow (forward part of the flat bottom,) it was making it a rough crossing. Because we were being towed, both engines were stopped and out of gear, the flow of water being forced against the props while being towed was turning the shafts and making a lot of noise, the engines were put into gear to stop the shafts turning. Great that stopped all the noise. Until about 2am, then there was a loud roar of an engine starting up. The rate of knots we were being towed must have turned the engine over and because it was in gear, made one of the engines to start!!

At dawn I could see the North African coast in the distance. *Warden* had winched us in, we were within hailing distance. We carried on for another hour or two passing many ships which were laying a few miles off Port Said. Finally, we said goodbye to *Warden*, (with instructions to proceed to the aircraft carrier HMS *Ocean*, and good luck.)

(Note: – HMS *Warden* then was on her way back to Cyprus to tow a heavy lift barge back to the area to help with the removal of the block ships.)

I have attached a photo of our arrival at Port Said the morning of the landings. The quality is not great, but you can see the naval ships on the horizon. Our Z craft is shown minus its ramp, removed, and welded to the deck, before leaving Cyprus for the tow over to Port Said, also a temporary

Fig 15 Tony Gathercole's Z craft being towed from Cyprus to the landings at Egypt by HMS *Warden*. The bow ramp has been welded to the deck. You can also just make out the convoy of warships in the background. (Photo, Tony Gathercole.)

Left: Fig 16 Another photograph taken by Tony, showing the Z craft out of commission but loaded with ammunition: 'I had to tow it 15 miles north of Port Said in the Med. to be dumped.'

Fig 17 Another photograph by Tony Gathercole, showing the tug *Helen K. Henges* ready to tow a barge full of old railway lines going to Port Said for scrap, from Fanara in the Bitter Lakes.

bow/breakwater welded to the deck to stop the sea washing all over the decks.

Our first job on arrival was to load Centurion tank ammunition, from HMS *Ocean*, to be taken to Abbas quay in the inner harbour past the block ships. The masts and funnels were not a problem, the underwater obstructions were, the Z craft had a shallow draft this helped, and we got through and delivered the ammunition.

I served my national service in 1952/54, I was posted to Egypt in the Canal Zone for 22 months. I was in the Royal Engineers my posting was to an IWT squadron in Ismailia by Lake Timsah on the canal. I was put on the tug Helen K. Henges as skipper a couple of months after my arrival. We worked from Adabiya Port in Suez Bay to Port Said, the length of the canal.

I have wondered about the *Helen K. Henges* but could never get any information about where she was built.

She did not have a plaque with the builder or year she was built. The only thing I heard was she was a Canadian lakes tug and going by the lines of her I think this is right.

While Tony Gathercole was going into Suez, the response of the American president, Dwight D. Eisenhower, was calm and measured. He warned the Soviets that reckless talk of nuclear conflict would only make matters worse, and he cautioned Khrushchev to keep out, and refrain from direct intervention in the conflict between the three aggressors and the Egyptians.

Fig 18 HMS *Newfoundland* (photo, Imperial War Museum).

Fig 19 The Leith-built River class frigate HMS *Nith* as the Egyptian navy's *Domiat*. (Image from naval-history.net, shown by permission of the late Gordon Smith.)

The fight for control of the Suez Canal was not only land-based; naval engagements were taking place as well, and one of those had involved the Leith-built River class frigate *Domiat*, which had been launched at the yard in September 1942 as HMS *Nith*, Ship No 327. The frigate was outgunned during an engagement on 31 October 1956. Pitched against the Royal Navy light cruiser HMS *Newfoundland* she was quickly left burning. *Domiat* was then sunk by *Newfoundland*'s escort, HMS *Diana*. Of the *Domiat*'s crew 38 were killed and 69 were rescued and survived. British losses in the engagement were 1 killed and 5 wounded. Then on 4 November, a squadron of Egyptian motor torpedo boats attacked a British destroyer off the north-east coast of the Nile delta. The attack was repelled, with three torpedo boats sunk and the rest retreating.

As the political sabre-rattling continued, the British and French forces continued fighting for control of the canal, along with the Israeli forces, who Britain had been fighting against only eight years earlier.

The American President Eisenhower (who had been commander in chief of all the Allied forces during the invasion of Europe in 1944) told the three invading countries to back off in no uncertain terms. He was still somewhat annoyed with Anthony Eden for not keeping America informed of the intentions of the three countries, and like a stern schoolmaster he threatened all three with heavy economic sanctions if they kept up this invasion. The threats were taken seriously, and the British and French had withdrawn from Egypt by December, with Israel finally bowing to American pressure in March 1957. Thus Egypt was able to regain control over the Suez Canal.

Partly as a consequence of this invasion, Britain and France found that their perceived previous influence in the world was waning, and they could no longer be seen as world powers. The real winner of this short bloody battle was the Egyptian leader Nasser, as he was suddenly propelled into being this powerful new leader and hero of the growing Arab and Egyptian nationalist movements. The Israelis did not gain the right to use the canal, although they were once again granted the right to ship goods through the Straits of Tiran, giving them maritime access to the Red Sea, hence directly to the Indian Ocean, the Far East and Australia.

Ten years later, with Arab nationalism at its height, the Egyptians closed the canal once more after their army had been routed in the short brutal six-day war with Israel in June 1967. It would be another decade before the Suez Canal could be used again, as the canal had been virtually the front line between the warring Egyptian and Israeli armies. So all shipping would have to take the old trade route around the Cape of Good Hope, giving rise to South Africa building the two largest and most powerful ocean-going salvage tugs in the world, one of them built at Leith launching in 1976 as SA *Wolraad Woltemade*.

Meanwhile in 1975, as a sign of goodwill and peace between Egypt and the West, the Egyptian president Anwar El-Sadat had reopened the Suez Canal to international shipping. At the time of writing it is estimated that 300–350 million tons of goods pass through the Suez Canal each year.

4: *BUSTLER*

His Majesty's Rescue Tug, HMRT *Bustler* was launched into the Firth of Forth on 4 December 1941, named by a Mrs Cooper. After some five months of fitting out and on completion of successful sea trials, *Bustler* was commissioned as a Royal Navy ship, and on receiving the pennant W 72 / A 240 was put straight to work in the Battle of the Atlantic.

She was involved in many daring rescues, including the rescue of *Empire Treasure* after she had lost her propeller; *Bustler* towed her over 1,900 nautical miles in gale-force winds to bring her safely back to port.

This fine old Leith-built vessel had a working life of close to 48 years, surviving the ravages of World War II. In peacetime, she reverted to salvage and towing work, chartered out to Metal Industries Ltd in 1946 to continue with the work of towing to

Fig 20 After the war was over the shipyard lost no time in advertising its prowess in building fine ships. As this advert shows, the yard was rightly proud of a fine record of building during the dark days of World War II. (The above advert is from an image I was sent many years ago, copyright unknown.)

scrapyards the large vessels deemed surplus to the war effort. In 1959, on being transferred to the Royal Fleet Auxiliary, she took the designation of RFA *Bustler*; she provided capable service until sold on in 1973 to continue with her salvage work, this time in Yugoslavia and renamed *Mocni*.

In 1975 she was renamed again, as *Smjeli*, and she was to continue working under this name until her eventual breaking up at Split in Yugoslavia in 1989.

Fig 21
RFA *Bustler*
looks in
need of some
paint in this
image from
RFA Plymouth.

HMRT *BUSTLER* – WAR SERVICE

As we have seen above, *Bustler*, Ship No 321, was finally, despite the interference of the Admiralty, launched on 4 December 1941; she was the lead ship in the eight-ship order of desperately needed vessels. This launch came a few days before the Japanese attack on Pearl Harbor, an event that would bring America into a war that had been raging in Europe for two years.

Once she had been successfully launched, she was taken in tow by the small Leith harbour tugs to go the short distance around the western pier to be moored amongst many others for her fitting out. At this stage she was but a shell of steel, complete with her mighty engines but lacking the necessities to turn her into a working ship.

This would now be the job carried out primarily by the finishing trades. Men from the engine shop, the plumbers' shop and joiners' shop would all be scrambling over her, with the electricians and all the other trades required to complete her ready for her trials, all fighting for space on the vessel. Men from the Black Squad would also be there to complete the steelwork jobs that had been left unfinished or had not been required to be completed before her launch. Week by week, the men would continue with their work; with a world war raging, every week going by meant another week that a convoy would cross the perilous Atlantic Ocean devoid of the required amount of rescue and salvage ships to aid the unfortunate crews of sunken vessels. *Bustler*'s galley was fitted out with a couple of very large cool stores, so that she could cater for up to 200 unfortunate mariners who might have ended up with their ship blown out from under them.

The following comes from the memories of Ernest Cooper, MBE CE FiMechE, who served his apprenticeship in the yard from 1941 to 1946. Who better qualified than he to tell the story of working in the Leith shipyards during wartime?

The blacksmiths shop was adjacent to the platers shop. Here steam hammers pounded into shape forgings, and white-hot iron swiftly taken from charcoal fires would be fused under these hammers to manufacture forged steel components. The boiler shop took plate of many sizes and often by hand hammer alone would be formed and cut. Above the platers was the 'loft', a great expanse of wooden floor, polished and clean but for the laths laid out to determine the frames for the construction of a ship on the slips. All work here was full size. To one side was a smaller space here was the pattern shop. Shelves and shelves of past made wooden patterns, all ready to go to the foundry when the need arose, were neatly stacked and referenced. Around were the woodworking tools.

Most memorable was that all this work used yellow pine. Today shipbuilding in the stocks is under cover but then all was in open air; wet or shine, cold or hot, work never stopped. Wooden structures surrounded a hull, scaffolding had yet to be developed. This was the time when ships were still plated and riveted, on these platforms high above the ground riveting gangs worked. The fire would be at ground level. Rivets ringed around the coals all in a heat sequence. By sound only the hottest rivet would be picked from the fire with tongs, then tossed many feet up to the 'catcher' to be then entered by the 'placer' into the hole in the plate for the 'backer' and 'knocker-up' to hammer into place.

All by hand, no pneumatics at that time, just considerable skill. Once the rivet had cooled it was swabbed with paraffin, if then there was the slightest sign of penetration on the other side the offending rivet would be replaced. Later this knowledge was of great help to me including the winning of a case of champagne in the Congo. Often rivets would be too long, while still red-hot they would be placed partially through the hole for the excess to be removed by a chisel.

You can imagine the noise of this activity inside the hull (a ship would be completely plated using bolts before riveting began) yet there were times when out of sight others and I would do our homework inside.

Bustler was ready for sea trials in early May, and she easily achieved her contract speed of 16 knots over the measured mile in the Firth of Forth.

On the successful completion of her trials she was ready for service in the Royal Navy; she was then sailed the short distance across the Forth to the huge naval base at Rosyth on the Fife coast, to receive her armament. She was commissioned into the Royal Navy on 14 May 1942; by the 27th she had left Rosyth for the short voyage down the firth to Methil, on the same coast.

She joined Convoy EN 90 to Oban, arriving on 29 May 1942 as HMRT *Bustler*. It is interesting to note that another Leith-built ship was with this convoy of 18 ships and 3 escort vessels: TSMV *Underwood*, built as Ship No 291 by Henry Robb and launched in January 1941. The convoy's code EN indicated that it was going from Methil around the top of Scotland to Oban. There its ships would split up and continue in some of the many other convoys to other destinations. From September 1942 she was operating out of Gibraltar, tasked with returning SS *Durham* to the UK. She would join what was to become the Campbeltown Navy from January 1943, operating out into the Atlantic before being ordered to Liverpool in early April.

On 6 April 1943 *Bustler* sailed from Liverpool in Convoy ON 177, bound for Halifax, Nova Scotia. This convoy consisted of some 20 merchant vessels with 16 escorts; most would go on to New York, arriving on 23 April.

Bustler was then moved from her duties in the Atlantic to working with the convoys from the Mediterranean, and in particular from Gibraltar, to the UK. Her first tow was on 23 June, when she was tasked with getting HMS *Manxman* safely back from Gibraltar. She was to be part of the Convoy MKS 15G from Gibraltar to Loch Ewe. (The designation MKS stood for 'slow convoy from the Mediterranean to Liverpool'.) The first 11 ships of the convoy would sail independently, and the fact that Bustler had a tow could only mean this would be a slow passage. So for its sailors this meant that contending with the unpredictable seas once in the Bay of Biscay, along with the dreaded U-boat threat off along the coasts of Portugal, Spain and France, all senses would be taut and on high alert.

At the end of 1943 *Durham*, a large and badly needed 14,000-ton merchant ship, was lying at Gibraltar with a big hole in her bows, most of her stern missing and other severe damage. It was *Bustler*'s job to get her back to England through 1,500 miles of water infested by U-boats. She set off with her charge, with a trawler and a corvette in attendance. Submarine attacks sometimes reached three in 24 hours, and in addition to fighting these off, the little convoy had to skirt around the British minefields. In the end, although the big ship, drawing 52 feet by the stern, was continually veering all over the place, the tow was successfully completed.

Bustler's commanding officer was then Lieutenant Commander E. Bond, RNR. Her later chief officer said, '*Bustler* is a fine ship and in our opinion the finest equipped and most comfortable ocean tug afloat.'

Although any towing work would be carried out at the slower speeds required to control a battered vessel under tow, once *Bustler*'s powerful engines were opened up, she was capable of sustaining 16 knots. This speed could mean the difference between life and death for sailors struggling to survive in the frigid waters that the convoys operated in. With rescue ships close by, at least the men had hope should the worst happen; without hope, all is lost.

The next episode of *Bustler*'s story was perhaps the most significant part of World War II, certainly in Europe. This was the planning and preparations for D-Day. While you will need no introduction to this momentous occasion, the invasion of Europe could not have been completed with any hope of success if the Allies could not supply the troops once they had landed on the beaches of Normandy.

Bustler was one of the tugs mainly responsible for towing the Conundrum, loaded with 1,500 tons of steel pipes, across the Channel in connection with the great Pluto operation for the invasion of Normandy. Model experiments at the National Physical Laboratory had indicated that the Bustler class was one of the only two types of tug which could provide the necessary power to achieve the desired operational laying speed of 5–6 knots.

Eventually it was found necessary to use two tugs, keeping station abreast of each other, for the longer distances, though from Dungeness to Boulogne only one tug was used.

Bustler was accompanied in the task of towing the vital petrol line across the Channel by HMS *Marauder*. This was a remarkable tow, which would have been impossible but for the immensely powerful tug that Henry Robb Shipbuilders had built for the Royal Navy.

Bustler, along with her sister *Samsonia*, would also tow some of the ships to be sunk as part of the breakwaters to help accommodate the massive concrete caissons that had been part-built and floated over the Channel to form the Mulberry harbours for ships to unload – yet another innovation by the Allies to help ensure that the troops could be supplied with the food and arms required for such an undertaking.

On 15 June 1944 *Bustler* sailed from Southend in Convoy ETC 10. (ETC indicated that the convoys were destined for France just after D-Day.)

Another Leith-built ship, HMS *Holdfast*, was deeply involved in the battle to lay and supply fuel to mainland France. She was the first Hais cable-laying ship. She had been converted from the Dundee, Perth & London Shipping Company's coastal passenger ship *London*, built in 1921 by Hawthorns & Co of Leith, and was 1,499 grt. Conversion commenced in the summer of 1942 and was completed later that year.

For her work in helping with the successful invasion of mainland Europe *Bustler* was awarded a well-deserved Normandy 1944 Battle Honour, to go with her Atlantic Battle Honour.

Fig 22 A Conundrum being towed across the English Channel, laying out pipe behind it to form an underwater pipeline from Southampton to Cherbourg. The tugs ahead are: *Bustler*, 3,200 ihp; *Marauder*, 3,000 ihp; and then *Danube V*, a smaller craft, astern of the two above, to facilitate steering of the tow. The pipeline kept the Allied armies supplied with petrol until the French channel ports could be reactivated. Known as Pluto, this was an entirely British concept. For more on Operation Pluto, see Chapter 3. (Image is T29 from the Imperial War Museum, via Wikipedia.)

The war in Europe ended on 8 May 1945, but the war in the Far East would go on until September. With the end of the conflict in Europe the work for the Bustler tugs would go on; for Operation Deadlight a great many U-boats needed to be towed from where they had been reported to surrender, many ending up in the lochs of Scotland to be destroyed.

On 9 December 1945 *Bustler* would sail from the large Loch Ryan, an area of sheltered water between Scotland and the unpredictable Atlantic. She was to tow the German type V11C/41 U997 from the loch to her eventual destination out of harm's way, to be used as a bombing target for the aircraft of the RAF's 248 Squadron. The aircraft made short work of U997, and she was sunk on 13 December 1945.

On 5 February 1946 *Bustler* sailed from Lisahally in Northern Ireland, towing the German submarine U2518 to Cherbourg during Operation Thankful. The Admiralty by this time had little work for *Bustler*, so she was chartered out to Metal Industries (Salvage) Ltd. at £6,000 per annum; this company had lots of work, as it was engaged in the salvage and breaking up of many of the wartime surplus vessels from both sides of the war just ended.

Then on 14 April *Bustler* was called to help with the rescue of RMS *Queen Elizabeth,* which had run aground in Southampton Water on the notorious Bramble bank, off the Bourne Gap buoy. *Bustler*, along with other tugs, helped to get the iconic liner floating safely once more, and for her part in this rescue operation the High Court would later award her the sum of £15,000. After Metal Industries had taken its cut of the salvage money, this award would be a nice bonus shared amongst her crew.

Bustler herself would require some help when on 16 November 1946 her engines stopped 15 miles off the Lizard and she was at the mercy of the elements. According to the story in the *Daily Herald* a message was flashed across the cinema screen to recall the men to their ship, the destroyer HMS *Wizard*, to stand by the tug.

From 1947 to 1958 she was chartered out for commercial use.

On 20 April 1947 *Bustler* was tasked with towing the old battleship HMS *Warspite* to her final resting place. *Bustler* and another tug, *Metinda III*, were to take *Warspite* from Portsmouth, where she had been stripped of her guns, up to the breaker's yard on the Clyde. The following day they were caught in a south-westerly gale and *Bustler*'s hawser

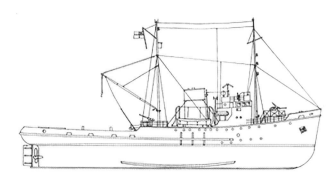

Fig 23 Sketch of the Bustler class rescue tug (image from Historical RFA).

snapped around 15 miles south of Wolf Rock Lighthouse. The storm raged on, and the three ships had been fighting it for 20 hours or so, as they drifted closer to the shore in Mounts Bay. By noon of that day *Metinda III* had to let go of the tow.

The 30,000-ton battleship had been driven about 30 miles in the raging seas and high winds. The Penlee lifeboat, which had come out, had to re-route to Newlyn harbour, as the seas were too rough to return to her base at the Penlee. As huge waves of 30 feet and more swept over the ship, she was being driven ever closer to the shore, and the rocks at Cudden Ledges, Prussia Cove. Just then the brave lifeboat crew arrived once more to attempt to help; they managed to manoeuvre the lifeboat into the narrow channel between the land and the ship, they then got two lines aboard the huge ship, as their small lifeboat bobbed up and down in 20-foot waves. The men could not stand upright on deck and had to crawl around holding onto anything that was close, the coxswain masterly cajoling the engines at full power, first ahead and then astern, just to keep on station and keep the lines on the ship.

The skeleton crew on *Warspite* dropped her anchor, but unfortunately it did not hold and the huge ship grounded around an hour later on Mountamopus Ledge, a mile to the south-west of Cudden Point. It took a long half-hour to get the skeleton crew and her captain off *Warspite* and back to the relative safety of Newlyn harbour. The storm had done more damage to *Warspite* than she had suffered during the two world wars; such is the power of nature.

It was decided to dismantle her where she lay on the shore; however, after she had been partially dismantled with her weight somewhat reduced, she was eventually towed by the two large salvage tugs *Englishman* and *Braham* to be beached at a more readily accessible part of the shore, at Marazion. It took a further ten years to demolish her, some parts being left where they can still be seen today.

Warspite was by no means the only battleship to be towed by the mighty *Bustler*, and not the last to give major problems.

THE LOST BATTLESHIP

A mystery of the vast deep oceans involved *Bustler*, involving the tow of the Brazilian battleship *São Paulo*.

After her use as battleship was over, *São Paulo* was used by the Brazilian navy as a training ship from 1947 to the summer of 1951. Finally, being deemed surplus to requirements the old ship was sold to the Iron and Steel Corporation of Great Britain. (BISCO), for scrap. During August 1951 she was prepared for her final journey to the breaker's yard in the UK. She was given an eight-man caretaker crew and taken under tow by two tugs, *Dexterous* and *Bustler*, in Rio de Janeiro on 20 September 1951 for her last voyage – to Greenock and the breakers.

But north of the Azores in early November, the two lines snapped during a strong storm. American B-17 Flying Fortresses and British planes were launched to scour the

Atlantic for the missing ship and on the 15th she was reported found, but this proved incorrect. The search was ended on 10 December without finding *São Paulo* or her crew. There is also a side to the story of the lost *São Paulo* which subscribes to the fact that perhaps she just disappeared, taken by aliens: some type of huge ray came along from a spaceship and whisked her away some place. As with all the great mysteries of the sea, perhaps we shall never know.

The book *Turmoil* by Ewart Brookes (Ch. 12) uses the incident to show the dangers inherent within towing jobs, yet rarely recalled.

The inquiry into the loss of the *São Paulo* was held at 10 Carlton House Terrace, London SW1, on 4–8 October 1954, before Mr R.F. Haywood QC, assisted by Captain A.M. Atkinson and Mr W.J. Nutton. They found no fault with the setting-up of the tow or the towing, but arrived at the conclusion that she had foundered, possibly capsizing, in a heavy north-westerly gale after the tow ropes of both tugs (*Dexterous* and *Bustler*) had parted. They put the loss down to 'the failure of the temporary closings of some gunports or other openings' – a job that had been entrusted to the Brazilian navy, though they discreetly never pointed any fingers in that direction.

Bustler was kept busy in the years after the loss of the *São Paulo*, including trips to Australia to help with the disposal of some out-of-date Australian warships.

In October 1956 she was tasked with towing HMAS *Lae* and HMAS *Labuan* from Sydney for delivery to the ship breakers at Hong Kong. Both ships had been fully loaded with scrap metal as part of the deal. In early November HMAS *Lae* broke her tow; she went aground on South Percy Island off the coast of Queensland, and was abandoned after an attempt to recover her cargo failed. She later sank.

Lae was a Landing Ship, Tank (L 3035) which had been built in Scotland by Denny of Dumbarton. She had been launched in 1944 and was transferred to the Australian Navy in 1946.

Some history on the Landing Ship, Tank HMAS *Labuan*: in 1947, LST 3501 had been selected to assist in the establishment and ongoing support of research facilities on Heard Island and Macquarie Island, both in the Southern Ocean. Painted yellow to assist with visibility in Antarctic waters, LST 3501 made her first trip to Heard Island in late 1947, landing scientists and their equipment before making a second trip, this time to Macquarie Island in February 1948. LST 3501 was renamed HMAS *Labuan* on 16 December 1948. She was paid off to the reserve on 28 September 1951 and sold for disposal on 9 November 1955.

A story tells of how *Bustler* brought back half of a tanker that had broken in two in the Bay of Biscay in March 1951. She managed to tow the stern half of the 10,000-ton tanker back to Falmouth.

She returned to the Southern Ocean islands five more times to deliver supplies and transfer personnel before being heavily damaged during a 1951 visit to Heard Island. Attempting to sail home, she broke down completely and had to be towed back to Fremantle.

Fig 24 This small sketch of *Bustler* was sent to me by Robert Rowbottom.

Another story from her time in Australian waters, originally printed in *The Argus*, Melbourne, of 1 August 1956, tells of when she was on a voyage from Melbourne to Hong Kong with two former Australian Navy corvettes, *Bowen* and *Latrobe*, to be scrapped; she towed them back to Brisbane on only one engine, the other one having packed it in some three days out of Brisbane.

HMRT *Bustler* was officially transferred to the Royal Fleet Auxiliary, with her name unchanged, in 1959, and under RFA conditions was to have a civilian crew.

In August 1960, along with her sister *Samsonia*, *Bustler* towed another great battleship, HMS *Vanguard*, from her base in Portsmouth to the breaker's yard at Faslane in Scotland.

Then in October 1962 *Bustler* was involved in a collision with the tug *Impetus* at Rosyth Naval Base in Fife. Six years later, while still going strong, she was involved in another collision, this time at Devonport Naval Base; there she collided with the Landing Ship, Tank (LST) HMS *Narvik* in March 1968.

One of her last jobs with the RFA was towing HMS *Zest* to the breaker's yard at Dalmuir, on the Clyde, in 1973.

Three months after towing *Zest* to the breakers *Bustler* was deemed to be surplus and she was sold to a commercial towing company in Yugoslavia. She was towed from Portsmouth by the Yugoslavian tug *Borak*. She was soon renamed *Mocni*, then in 1975 renamed *Smjeli*. She would go on to continue doing what she had been designed and built for until she met the inevitable and was scrapped by her owners in Split, Yugoslavia, in 1989.

So ended the career of a fine, solid ship. She had served for 48 years. She must have saved a great many lives, not to mention thousands of tonnes of shipping.

Left: Fig 25 RFA *Bustler* as the renamed Yugoslav *Smjeli* (image from Historical RFA website).

Lower: Fig 26 Two mighty warriors together: HMRT *Bustler* and HMRT *Samsonia*, ex-*Samson* (image from RFA Plymouth).

While I ran my website on the ships built at Leith, where a lot of the source information of the book originates, it was always a pleasure to see so many of the people connected with the tugs writing in to the website with some splendid comments. I think it is only fitting that rather than have these comments lost to history I should feature them in this book, so here they are:

Richard Codd

My father John Codd served on the *Bustler* during ww2. Stories include attempting rescue of HMS Ark Royal off Gibraltar and towing HMS *Manxman* after she had been torpedoed.

Ray Gill

I sailed on the *Bustler* in 1967 with Philpots and Burt the cook and Joe Dixon

William Henderson

while surfing the web I came across two Tugs built by Henry Robb Shipbuilders Leith the *Bustler* and the *Samsonia*. My father served on both of these Tugs during the last war, first the B 1940 the S in 1941 which he remained on till the end of the war, many a story he could tell on the great Tows the ships were involved in. His name was as follows P O Thomas Henderson, sorry I have no mementos except a photo of him in his uniform---------Bill Henderson

5: *SAMSON/SAMSONIA*

As the war moved into 1942, with the Americans now deciding they could not stay neutral any more after being attacked by the Japanese, the shipyard at Leith was working flat out to supply the orders that they had received. Included in the order book was *Bustler*'s sister ship, along with the other two rescue tugs that had been ordered.

HMRT *Samson*, Ship No 322, was launched from the yard on 1 April 1942, 14 months after her keel had been laid, by the Hon. Mrs W.S. Carson. *Samson* was then towed around to the fitting-out basin for completion before going on her sea trials. On successful completion of her trials, she was soon commissioned, and received pennant W 23 on 14 September 1942.

Without interference from the Admiralty causing delays, her build and outfitting was completed in between the build of the warships. With many of the problems ironed out in the build of the lead ship this system was not unusual in a shipyard. She was laid down as HMS *Samson* which was changed to HMS *Samsonia* at her launching. Her name was certainly fitting, as she would go onto take part in a great many endurance tests in the unpredictable seas around the world.

By 6 October *Samsonia* was ready to take up her role as a convoy salvage/rescue ship, and she sailed from Methil in Convoy EN 146/2, arriving at Loch Ewe on 9 October. From early 1943 she was based at Campbeltown as a convoy rescue tug.

By late February 1943 *Samsonia* was to be found in warmer climes as she took over towing duties from HM Tug *Nimble*. *Samsonia*'s job was to tow SS *Ariguani* from Gibraltar to Greenock. *Samsonia* then sailed on to the Tyne, arriving 22 March 1943, while Nimble returned to Gibraltar.

Work would never cease for the big tug, she was called to a salvage job in late March, involving a ship that had been hit by torpedoes and all of her crew had abandoned ship.

As if to emphasise the fickle hand of fate, her crew had abandoned her when *Samsonia* got to her along with the tug *Eminent* she was still afloat and the two tugs were able to take her in tow, back to the Clyde.

When you look at the image shown from recently released documents from the U.S. Navy in Washington D.C. you will read the commanding officers of the escort ship *USCGC*

Fig 27 *Samsonia* with a foredeck gun on 24 February 1943 at Greenock. One of the world's largest tugs, she had just completed her task of towing HMS *Ariguani*, a fighter catapult ship, nearly 1,400 miles from Gibraltar. (Image from Historical RFA Gallery.)

Fig-zz- US Navy report on the events leading up to and after SS *Coulmore* had been hit by a torpedo.

CONFIDENTIAL

NAVY DEPARTMENT
Op-16-B-5   OFFICE OF THE CHIEF OF NAVAL OPERATIONS   April 29, 1943
WASHINGTON

MEMORANDUM FOR FILE

SUBJECT: Summary of Statements by Survivors SS COULMORE, British
Freighter, 3670 G.T., owners Lambert Bros. Shipping Co.

1.   The COULMORE was torpedoed without warning at 0010 GCT, on
March 10, 1943 in 58.48 N - 22.00 W, having sailed from New York in convoy
SC-121 on February 23, 1943 for Hull, England with a general cargo of sulphite and phosphates, draft forward 25', aft 23'. The ship was still afloat
at 1400 GCT, March 11 in 58.30 N - 19.31 W, and was eventually taken in tow
arriving at Clyde, England March 20th.

2.   The ship was on course 096° T., speed 7.25 knots, not zigzagging, blacked out, radio last used March 5, 1943, 4 lookouts - port and
starboard Oerlikon nests, 1 forward gun platform, 1 after gun platform.
Weather overcast, sea with swells, wind WSW, force - 6, no moonlight, visibility 4000 yards, other ships of convoy in sight.

3.   At 0010 GCT a torpedo struck on port side below break of
forecastle house and exploded in chain locker. Ship was holed through and
through at bow forward of No. 1 bulkhead, flooding was slow. Main engines
were secured prior to abandonment. Distress signal sent, no reply received.
No counter offensive offered. Disposition of confidentials unknown.

4.   After the explosion was heard, crew members immediately
gathered aft and commenced lowering away the lifeboats without orders. The
port boat was lowered; 14 persons got in and found no tiller to be fitted to
the rudder. Additional confusion arose from the fact that part of the occupants were facing toward the bow and the remainder toward the stern. An
attempt was made to try to pull away from ship and place bow to the sea, boat
swamped and occupants were thrown into the sea. Some made their way to an
unoccupied life raft and others were not seen again. Five other crew members
went forward and released a raft, which they boarded by means of a line down
from the deck. Five survivors were picked up by the USCG B133 and landed
at Reykjavik on March 15. Total crew on board was 41; five men saved, 13 are
known dead and 23 are missing and presumed lost.

5.   Submarine not sighted at any time.

6.   It is stated that had the crew remained on board, the ship
could have been saved and disastrous loss of life avoided. At 1400 GCT, March
11 the COULMORE was seen from the rescue ship riding high in the water with
every appearance of seaworthiness and stability. All too frequently it is
necessary to sink derelicts by gunfire many hours after they have been struck
due to crew abandonment before inspection of damage.

NOTE: Other ships attacked in convoy SC-121 were the MALANTIC,
NAILSEA COURT, FORT LAMY, EGYPTIAN, GUIDO, COULMORE, VOJVODA
PUTNIK, and ROSEWOOD. The LEADGATE, EMPIRE IMPALA, EMPIRE
LAKELAND and MILOS are missing and presumed lost.
ROBERT G. FULTON
Lt. (jg) U.S.N.R.

CC: ONI B-2, 16-B-2, 16-FP(Ensign Judd), 16-P-1, 16-Z(5 copies), Cominch,
Cominch F-21-22, F-25(ASWORG) (Dr. Gishen, Rm.4307), F-37(Gen), F-252, F-353,
Op-20-G-M, Op-23-L,   Op-30, Op-39(2 copies), BuShips, BuOrd(Re-6-a), BuOrd,
Atlantic Fleet Anti-Sub Unit, BuPers 222,222-23, CG(2 copies), DIO 1,3,4,5,6,
7(3 copies), 8,10(4 copies), 11(3 copies), 12,13,14(4 copies) 15 MD's, Coord.

Fig-yy *SS Coulmore* as an armed merchantman during WW2

Bibb, and it shows a story of extreme sadness. Easy to say now many years after the fact that the men would have been better and perhaps would have survived had they stayed with the vessel. Civilian crews that had been living on the edge with every trip taken knowing full well that they may end up in the periscope sights of an enemy submarine.

The report from the US would tend to indicate that the abandoned *Coulmore* was not an isolated incident and as I say above who knows how anyone may have reacted in these very dark days of World War Two in the North Atlantic.

SS Coulmore had been hit by U-229 when the Germans attacked convoy SC 121 just south of Reykjavik, Iceland on 10th March, the order was given to abandon ship. The lifeboats lowered but one lifeboat was swept away before anyone could get aboard, the other lifeboat was swamped drowning all the occupants. Only 7 survivors from her crew of 47 were picked up, 2 by *HMCS Dauphin* and 5 by the *USCGC Bibb*.

Samsonia and *Eminent* arrived at the ship after being ordered to salve her on March 23rd, they proceeded to tow the vessel back to the Clyde in Scotland for repairs, and she returned to service in the July of 1943.

The ship was put to good use once repaired then in 1948 her owners sold her and she was renamed to *SS Avisford*, then in 1950 sold on once more with the new name of *SS Stripa*, she was further named after being sold in 1957 to SS Nautic, sailing under this name until 1966 when she was renamed SS Saratoga. The ship would eventually go for breaking up in 1969.

In April, while the tug was covering in the Atlantic, she received a rather strange request. At first her officers were unsure that the message was correct: they were to look for a Lockheed bomber.

Sure, enough the message was correct: after a few hours of searching in the designated area the crew spotted a Lockheed bomber standing upright, strapped to a huge wooden raft. The raft had been tied down onto the deck of a merchant ship that had been torpedoed. As the ship sank, the raft had become detached and had floated away from the ship.

The tug duly took the raft with its precious cargo under tow; with some difficulty she managed to bring the plane back to the UK. This unusual tow took *Samsonia* three days, but the plane was delivered with only a dent in her nose.

The next day, 24 April, orders were received from the Admiralty to sail to St John's, Newfoundland, under the escort of HMS *Northern Sun*.

In May, her commanding officer was Lieutenant Commander Owen Jones OBE RNR, previously with the well-known towing firm United Towing Co., Hull.

The big tug was becoming well known for her exploits, with press reports around the English-speaking world. On 26 May 1943 the *Hull Daily News* reported the tale of the 1,400-mile tow of SS *Ariguani* along with the strange tow of the Lockheed bomber.

On 6 June 1943 *Samsonia* sailed from Campbeltown to Greenock for repairs to her No 2 engine. On 22 June it was time for her to sail from Campbeltown to Greenock again, for inspection of her engines. She arrived at Greenock the following day – and then in July she was back in the Atlantic again, picking up a tow from the large HX 247 convoy from Halifax to Liverpool. On 19 August she sailed from her base in Campbeltown, headed for the Moville anchorage in Lough Foyle, Northern Ireland.

As the New Year of 1944 began, it was work as usual for *Samsonia* when she was given orders to sail from Campbeltown to assist SS *Barendrecht*, in ballast and aground in Wigtown Bay about 2 miles north-east of Burrow Head; she had been holed fore and aft. She was refloated and towed to Liverpool.

Fig 28 SS *Barendrecht* (image from Historical RFA Gallery).

Fig 29 HMS *Samsonia* (image from Historical RFA Gallery).

Fig 30 Hat band (image from Historical RFA Gallery).

H.M.S. SAMSONIA

Towards the end of January *Samsonia* was anchored at Lough Foyle, having sailed on 23 January from Campbeltown. She was in the lough to meet up with a large convoy there: ON 221 from Liverpool to New York. This convoy would run into very bad weather, with many of its 74 vessels receiving hull damage.

In February 1944, her commanding officer was Lieutenant Commander Archibald M. Leekie, RNR. *Samsonia* was berthed at St. John's, Newfoundland, on 6 February and by the 9th she had sailed from St. Johns with HMS *Gentian* and SS *Kelmscott* to join the escorted Convoy HX 278 in the swept channel. But *Kelmscott* hit mines – no less than four explosions were heard – and once she had settled back in the water *Samsonia* was able to get a tow on her and bring her safely back to St. John's.

That same busy month *Samsonia* took HMS *Hart* in tow after that ship had fouled her propellers with replenishment at sea (RAS) gear.

The following month *Samsonia* was assigned as rescue tug to Convoy JH 97 sailing from St. John's to Halifax, leaving St. John's on 7 March 1944, arriving at Halifax on the 10th. Then on 3 May, escorted by HMS *Cam* and HMS *Lochy*, she towed the torpedoed USS *Donnell* (DE 56) from a point 450 miles south-west of Cape Clear, the most southerly point of the Irish mainland, to Dunstaffnage Bay, western Scotland, arriving on 12 May.

If the first six months of 1944 had been a busy time for *Samsonia*, the following months were to be ones that determined the eventual outcome of the war in Europe. The invasion of Normandy was to start in early June, with *Samsonia* and her sister *Growler*, along with

Fig 31 USS *Donnell*, DE 56 (photo from Navsource.org).

Left: Fig 32 The old French battleship *Courbet* (image from Historical RFA).

Right: Fig 33 A line of Phoenix caisson units, complete with anti-aircraft guns, forming part of a Mulberry harbour. (Image taken from the blog at 'Think Defence', copyright unknown.)

many more tugs, fully occupied with the lead-up to, and consolidation of, the Allied forces as they landed on the beaches of Normandy.

She would be in action on 7 June, the day after D-Day, when she sailed from Weymouth with HMRT *Growler*, towing the old French battleship *Courbet*, whose engines and guns had been removed and replaced with many tons of concrete; she would be sunk to act as a Gooseberry breakwater at Sword Beach during the Battle of Normandy, along with another eight blockships, all to be placed before the Mulberry harbours were assembled.

Courbet, at 25,000 grt, had been the lead ship of her class of four dreadnoughts. She had been completed in August 1914, and shad spent World War I in the Mediterranean, where she had helped to sink an Austro-Hungarian cruiser, covered the Otranto Barrage which bottled up the Austro-Hungarian navy in the Adriatic Sea, and often served as a flagship. But by World War II she was long obsolete, used by the Free French Navy as a stationary anti-aircraft battery in Portsmouth until she was turned into a Gooseberry. After the war she was scrapped where she lay.

Mulberry was the codename for the many and various structures that would make up the artificial harbours. Two would be built: one for the Americans, Mulberry A, approximately the size of Dover harbour, and one for the British/Canadian forces, Mulberry B. When a huge storm hit the region on 19 June, Mulberry A was put out of action; Mulberry B, however, continued in use until November 1945, six months after the war had ended.

There were six different sizes of caisson (with displacements of approximately 2,000 to 6,000 tons.) Having been sunk off the coast of southern England after manufacture to keep them hidden, they were refloated for the tow to France. Each unit was towed across the Channel at a speed of around 3 knots.

The Bustler class vessels were used to tow some of the Mulberry harbour caisson units to France, and on 15 June *Samsonia* arrived at Mulberry A, towing a Phoenix Unit 21/A1.

All through July *Samsonia* was on convoy duties as the ships with stores and men streamed back and forth across the Channel; she sailed on 2 July in Convoy FTC 24 from

Seine Bay to arrive at Southend the following day. She then sailed from Portsmouth on the 10th, joining Convoy FTC 32 for Southend; this convoy, once more arriving the following day, also contained HMRT *Bustler*, along with HMS *Saucy*.

Samsonia's next trip involved a round voyage from Portsmouth on 24 July, joining Convoy FTC 45 and arriving back at Portsmouth on the 29th.

The same day she sailed from Seine Bay to Southend as part of Convoy FTM 52. She then sailed from Seine Bay in Convoy FTM 57 on 2 August to arrive at Southend on the 3rd.

In the final year of this long war she was back on Atlantic convoy duty. On 23 January 1945 she was sailing from Liverpool in the escorted Convoy ON 280 as a rescue tug, then detached from the convoy on the 27th.

On 11 April she passed Gibraltar with RFA *Envoy*, towing the Admiralty Floating Dock (AFD) 32 from America via San Juan, Puerto Rico, on the way to Oran; by the 13th she had been joined by HMRT *Mediator*, another Henry Robb-built tug of the Bustler class; the floating dock was now under the control of three tugs.

On her way back from Oran she joined Convoy MKF 43 sailing from Gibraltar on 29 April and arriving in Liverpool just a couple of days before the war in Europe was to end.

In June 1945 she helped to remove the Phoenix units from France, almost a year after towing them there; they were now on the way back to the UK. November 1945 found her sailing from Le Havre Roads with *Ole Weggar* in tow, bound for Falmouth. She was escorted by HMRT *Erner* and HMRT *Emire Pixie*, along with the American salvage vessel *American Salvor*.

Wartime had been very eventful for *Samsonia*; she had been through a lot in the five years since her launch at Leith. Peacetime would, however, mean that there would not be so much work to go around, so in January 1947 *Samsonia* was chartered out to a Canadian salvage company, Foundation Maritime Ltd of Halifax, Nova Scotia, which would have been well aware of these fine ships' capabilities; *Samsonia*, renamed *Foundation Josephine*,

Fig 34 As *Foundation Josephine* when chartered out. (Image from Haze Gray.org, with permission by Sandy McClearn.)

was involved in many adventures, and there was even a book, *The Serpent's Coil*, written about her by Farley Mowat. She was soon put to work by the Canadians, and on 14 June she was recorded as passing the Lloyds Signal Station sailing east with SS *Edward E. Sparford* in tow.

By September 1947, while on passage from St. John's, Newfoundland, to Halifax she was diverted to assist in the salvage of the freighter *Mont Sorrel*, which had run aground on Cerberus Rock, unfortunately located at the entrance to the Strait of Canso, 120 miles east of Halifax. The vessel was successfully refloated three days later, with an RCMP (Royal Canadian Mounted Police) cutter also standing by.

On 14 September 1948, SS *Leicester* was abandoned by her crew in hurricane force winds some 200 miles south of Cape Race, Newfoundland. By the time *Foundation Josephine* had managed to locate her, she was listing badly and had drifted a long way; she was now 800 miles from both Bermuda and St. John's Newfoundland, 900 miles from Halifax, and 1,100 miles from New York. On 27 September 1948, a line was connected to *Leicester* with some difficulty, and the challenging tow to Bermuda commenced. Then on 9 October, during another heavy storm, *Foundation Josephine* was blown onto Ferry Point, Bermuda, while *Leicester* was blown into Whalebone Bay. It took until 22 October before *Foundation Josephine* was refloated, and she was then towed back up to Halifax, Nova Scotia, entering dry dock there for three months of repairs.

Once the repairs were finished, on 18 November, she was back ready for duty, and just two days later she sailed from Sydney, Nova Scotia, to the aid of the 4,200-ton Panamanian-registered *Evgenia*, which had lost her steering some 800 miles south-east of Halifax. *Foundation Josephine* successfully towed the crippled ship back to Halifax.

The following year, with November storms once more in the news, *Foundation Josephine* was called to the aid of yet another ship, the British-registered freighter *Scottish Prince* 7,138 grt, broken down in the heavy swell of the Atlantic around 700 miles east of Newfoundland.

Fig 35 *Foundation Josephine* on the rocks in Bermuda (from an image courtesy of Mel Clark).

In early February 1950 *Foundation Josephine* sailed out of Halifax bound for the Norwegian-registered freighter *Gudvor*, another vessel in trouble some 500 miles east of Newfoundland; she was taking in water and had little steering way with defective gear.

In situations such as this ex-*Samsonia*'s top speed was critical, enabling her to be on the scene as fast as possible. Not only in the hope of saving lives, but also to maximise the chances of claiming salvage rights, as many other deep sea tugs were in the same game; the first of them to the victim was the one who claimed the prize.

Looking for business in September 1951, the cold North Atlantic was her playground now. After the depths of winter, February in the Atlantic is still noted for bad weather, and that month in 1952 would prove a busy time for the ship.

Foundation Josephine's first call-out that month was to *Industria*, in trouble around 900 miles east of Bermuda; on 4 February she had lost her stern post and rudder. *Foundation Josephine* had her in tow by the following day, and by the 8th had taken her into Newport News, Virginia.

On 18 February 1952, the New England coast was hammered by a fierce storm, generating waves that topped 70 feet. Two 500-foot tankers, *Fort Mercer* and *Pendleton*, had been broken in half by the heavy seas just off Cape Cod. They had been built under the Emergency Powers Act in America during World War II, when quantity preceded quality. They were T2-SE-A1 designs, well known for breaking in two, partly due to poor welding and poor workmanship.

Pendleton got the Hollywood treatment some 50 years later as the action was turned into the movie called *The Finest Hours*, although the film, ignoring the role of *Foundation Josephine*, dealt only with the sinking of the *Pendleton* and the amazing work of the US Coast Guard in rescuing most of the men from the two stricken vessels.

At midday on 18 February, *Fort Mercer*, with her cargo of full of kerosene and fuel oil, first cracked, then broke completely into two halves, approximately 30 miles east of Chatham, Massachusetts. Her captain, Frederick Paetzel, radioed for help, reporting that near-70-foot waves were hitting her. When she broke into two, nine officers and crew were stranded in the bow section, while her remaining 34 crew were in the stern section, with the radio and engine still working. The US Coast Guard vessels *Eastwind* and *Unimak*, which were about 120 miles away near Nantucket, Massachusetts, headed to her. They reached the bow section while two more US Coast Guard cutters headed for the stern.

A Coast Guard PBY (patrol bomber) aircraft out of Coast Guard Air Station Salem was sent to look for the ship, but could not find her. The Coast Guard vessels *Yakutat* and *Acushnet*, eventually with the use of life-rafts and surfboats, rescued the men while many of the 34 men jumped from the stern section onto the Coast Guard cutter *Acushnet*.

But 13 men refused to leave the stern section; it still had electricity and plenty of food. When *Foundation Josephine* arrived and the seas had calmed down a bit, some of the rescuers who went on board the stern were treated to a breakfast of bacon and eggs.

Fig 36 Crew of the USCGC *Yakutat* pull in a life-raft carrying survivors from *Fort Mercer*'s bow section; the photo was taken 20 minutes prior to its sinking in the aftermath of the storm. (Image from Wikipedia-USCG photograph.)

Left: Fig 37 *Samsonia*, renamed *Foundation Josephine*, in Halifax, Nova Scotia, chartered to the Canadians, with winter ice building up as she ties up at the wharf. (Shown here by kind permission of Sandy McClearn, who runs the wonderful Haze Gray website in Canada.)

Right: Fig 38 *Foundation Josephine*, on the right, at her wharf once more in Halifax, Nova Scotia (also shown here by kind permission of Sandy McClearn).

Fig 39 RFA *Samsonia*: with her low flat stern and sweeping sheer line going forward, this ship just looked right. Like a powerful dog that would strain any leash, she was more than capable. (Image from Historical RFA.)

Five members of *Fort Mercer's* 43-man crew were lost, trapped in the sinking bow. But her stern section, which remained afloat, was towed to Newport, Rhode Island, by *Foundation Josephine*, to be outfitted with a new bow and rechristened *San Jacinto*. The new ship was 41 feet longer than *Fort Mercer* and had 29 tanks instead of 26.

The ship split in half again, however, in 1964 and again was rebuilt, this time renamed *The Pasadena*. She was partially salvaged, then scrapped in 1983.

On the end of her charter to Foundation Towing of Canada, the ship was returned to the Admiralty on 17 November 1952, renamed HMS *Samsonia*, and given the pennant number A 218.

HMS SAMSONIA

HMS *Samsonia* was stationed in the UK until August 1956, when her captain received a secret signal from the Admiralty via Commander-in-Chief Portsmouth, that she, along with another Bustler class vessel, RFA *Warden*, should tow Lifting Craft 10 and 11 from the UK to Malta. The lifting craft would have civilian crews, and on arrival at Malta both tugs would remain temporarily based in the Mediterranean. At this time events were running up to the Suez Crisis, which would begin in October 1956, so the whole of the eastern Mediterranean was on edge. On 22 September *Samsonia* entered Valletta's Grand Harbour, but she would not be involved in the conflict.

By 1958, with the Suez Crisis well over, *Samsonia* was to find herself back home based at Portsmouth, where she was put to use towing HMS *Mermaid* to the River Tyne. Two days later she was berthed alongside Bergen Quay on this famous old river, and the following day she departed the Tyne for Devonport. She was to sail once more to the Tyne, with HMS *Hart* in tow, reaching the river on 24 January 1958; she tied up alongside Palmer's Shipyard at Jarrow, then later that same day sailed for Portsmouth.

Her next job was a big one, and one that would end up in the record books. She was now in the warm waters of the Caribbean with orders to tow the submarine HMS *Turpin*, which had engine problems, from Kingston, Jamaica, to Devonport for urgent repairs. She would undertake this tow via the Canary Islands. The tow of HMS *Turpin* for some 5,200 miles took 29½ days, becoming the longest tow in submarine history; they left Kingston in March to arrive at Devonport on 8 April 1958

In the September *Samsonia* towed the destroyer HMS *Childers* to Gibraltar to be laid up, then it was back to Portsmouth, where she could be found berthed beside HMS *Warden*. The following year began with the tow of another Admiralty Floating Dock (AFD 26) from Portland to Portsmouth. Later the same year she was in collision with HMS *Hardy* at Portsmouth, then in May 1960 she was transferred to the Royal Fleet Auxiliary.

She would now be renamed RFA *Samsonia*, with Captain J.B. Gibson, MBE, appointed as her master. Three months later she was towing the obsolete battleship HMS *Vanguard* from Portsmouth to the ship breakers at Faslane on the Clyde, sharing the tow with her sister ship, RFA *Bustler*. In this book's foreword you will have read a snippet of an insight into what First Lieutenant Day thought of the botched start to this journey.

Then another Admiralty Floating Dock (AFD No 59) required moving, along with the tugs *Capable* and RFA *Agile*, from Portsmouth to Barrow-in-Furness, to be used as a fitting-out berth for the new atomic-powered submarines. The next few years would see *Samsonia* berthed around Devonport, moving in and out of Plymouth Sound along with RFA *Bustler*. It would be August 1962 before *Samsonia* was to be found back in the warmer waters around Malta, where she had sailed to from Rosyth.

A few months later she was back in Scotland; this time she caused some damage to the Princess Pier at Greenock – but no great harm done, and she sailed for Devonport once more, to carry out her usual duties of salvage and rescue of vessels and men at sea. Along with RFA *Typhoon*, another Henry Robb-built tug from a later year than the Bustler class, *Samsonia* was to tow the 8,000-ton obsolete monitor ship HMS *Roberts* to the scrapyard. The tow would begin at Devonport on 19 July 1965, finishing at the yard at Inverkeithing, just along the road from Rosyth. The two tugs towing *Roberts* would pass Leith on the way down the Firth of Forth, to arrive at the breakers on 3 August.

HMS *Roberts* was a Royal Navy Roberts-class monitor from World War II. Built by John Brown & Company of Clydebank, she had been laid down on 30 April 1940, launched on 1 April 1941 and completed on 27 October. She had reused the twin 15-inch gun turret of the World War I monitor *Marshal Soult*, and she provided bombardment support during Operation Torch, the invasion of North Africa. She was involved in the invasion of Sicily, then the Allied landings at Salerno, before her participation in the D-Day landings. Then she was used to help retake the Port of Antwerp, which was guarded by a heavily armoured fortress on Walcheren, the most seaward island of the Rhine delta.

In July 1945, *Roberts* departed the United Kingdom for the Indian Ocean to support the operation for the planned liberation of Singapore. But at the time of the Japanese surrender on 15 August she had only got as far as Port Said.

Left: Fig 40 HMS *Roberts* (image from Historical RFA).

Right: Fig 41 HMS *Victorious* around 1959, with her new angled flight deck, allowing her to accommodate faster and heavier aircraft. (Image from the US Navy National Museum of Naval Aviation.)

One of *Roberts'* guns (originally from the battleship *Resolution*) is mounted outside the Imperial War Museum in London, together with one from the battleship *Ramillies*.

A lot of *Samsonia's* work would now be taking many well-known Royal Navy ships to be broken up in Scotland, where many of them had started out. *Samsonia* worked in tandem many times with tugs that had been built in the yard where she had been laid down.

In January 1967, working with RFA *Typhoon* once more, she towed HMS *Sheffield* from Portsmouth to the naval dockyard at Rosyth. Then the following year she was involved in another collision, this time with HMS *Sirius* at Portsmouth. In July 1968 she sailed from Portsmouth, towing, along with RFA *Reward* and RFA *Agile*, the 30,000-ton aircraft carrier HMS *Victorious*. They were heading for the breaker's yard at Faslane. They left Portsmouth on the 11th, arriving at the yard on the 16th.

Then she had the unusual job, during the Troubles in October 1969, of towing HMS *Maidstone* to Belfast, to be moored there and used for confining prisoners under army control.

As she was returning from delivering *Maidstone*, while sailing past the Isles of Scilly she was sent to provide assistance to the Canadian destroyer HMCS *Kootenay*, which had suffered an engine room explosion some 200 miles off Plymouth killing eight men, with a further nine injured (one of whom would later die). *Samsonia* towed the stricken ship back to the UK.

Very soon after that she was on her way from Devonport to the Tyne with the submarine HMS *Astute* in tow, destined for the breaker's yard at Dunston. The following October, 1970, she was in the far north of Scotland with HMS *Stalker* in tow, when she suffered a mechanical breakdown in bad weather in the Pentland Firth. She limped back to port for repairs before being laid up for a couple of years.

Fig 42 The rescue tug RFA *Samsonia* (photo courtesy of RFA Plymouth).

Fig 43 *Samsonia* W23, later A218 (photo A. Hughes collection).

As time moved on *Samsonia* was deemed surplus to requirements, and on 25 August 1973 she was offered up for sale. With no takers, she was offered for sale again in September, sold as is while lying at Devonport Dockyard.

By February 1974 she had been purchased by the Yugoslavian company Brodospas-Brodus Split, Salvage, Towage and Demolition Enterprises, and renamed *Jaki* – she was to be refitted on the Tyne.

She was to work out of her new home base at Split for another five years, then on 11 May 1979 she was deleted from the register and laid up at Sveti while her parts were taken from her to be fitted onto *Bustler*, which had been purchased by the same company and renamed *Smjeli*. Then in September 1987 *Jaki,* ex-*Samsonia*, was finally broken up by her owners.

This was remarkable longevity for any vessel, let alone a very hard-working deep sea ocean-going tug. She was a fine testimony to the men who had built her and the men who sailed on her.

The following story was sent to me by W. Henderson, son of Chief Petty Officer Thomas Henderson:

Fig 44 CPO T. Henderson, who served on HMRT *Bustler* and HMRT *Samsonia* (image sent to me by his son, W. Henderson).

HMRT *Bustler* and HMRT *Samsonia*

My father Thomas Henderson served on both of these ships 1941 to 1945.

He was first on *Bustler* from her build in 1941 then transferred to *Samsonia* in 1942. He was originally in the Merchant Navy. Born in Leith, he married my mother Helen who had four children, one girl and three boys. After surviving the war, he moved to Australia,

My father's name was Thomas Henderson; he held the rank

of Chief Petty Officer. The only tow that the family can remember was the *Durham Castle* liner –sunk by a Mine while on Tow about early 1940s.

The man in command was Lieutenant Commander Ralph Kimber MBEM, Royal Navy – look up Newspaper London Gazette 1946.

George MacDonald also contacted me to say that his father had served on *Samsonia* from 1943 to 1946, and he told me that his father had many fond memories of his time on *Samsonia*:

George Macdonald

My late father passed away last November 2011, aged 86 years old, sailed on H.M.S *Samsonia* from 43-46, had many fond memories on and of her.

6: *GROWLER AND HESPERIA*

HMRT *GROWLER*

The keel for the next in line of the Bustler class was laid down at Leith on 31 January 1942. She would be Ship No 328 in the Henry Robb Shipyard order book.

After an eight-month build, she was ready for launching on 10 September 1942. The lady given the honour of carrying out the launching ceremony was Mrs Colin Sarel, and the ship was duly named HMRT *Growler*. What a great name for a deep sea rescue/salvage tug!

She had a five-month fitting-out period including her successful sea trials, and she was commissioned into the Royal Navy on 16 March 1943, just as the Battle of the Atlantic was about to enter its deadliest phase. Two days after her commission she sailed from Methil in Convoy EN 206 arriving at Loch Ewe on 20 March. After that whirlwind start, the year 1943 was to provide little respite for *Growler* and her crew.

One month later she was sent with all speed to help SS *Lena Luckenbach*, which had been in collision with another ship; she had been holed badly and was in danger of sinking. The ship had been struggling to reach Londonderry but her crew had abandoned her, taking passage on SS *Lightning* to Liverpool. Rescue tug *Growler* reached the vessel and managed to secure a tow.

Fig 45 SS *Lena Luckenbach* (image from Historical RFA).

On 30 April *Growler* sailed from Liverpool, to join Convoy ON 181 to New York on 1 May. Eight days into this perilous voyage she was called to the rescue of HMS *Daneman*, an escort trawler that was taking water into her engine room and boiler; she had no power as *Growler* took her in tow. But the following day the tow parted; 31 of the crew were saved by *Growler* while 13 others were picked up by the French ship FS *Renoncule*, but unfortunately by then two of *Daneman's* men were dead and four were missing, never to be recovered.

Growler was on the return convoy, HX 239, from New York as rescue tug, then the next month she sailed from the Clyde to Londonderry, towing LST (Landing Ship, Tank) 406. By 28 October she was once more on convoy duty, joining Convoy MKS 27G which had left Gibraltar on the 14th; she was to help provide the escort for the convoy's voyage to Liverpool.

The day before Christmas 1943 she sailed from Campbeltown to Moville to rendezvous with an outbound convoy which had set out on Christmas Day. But on the 30th she was accidentally rammed by the tanker *Donna Bella*. Although severely damaged, she managed to make it to Iceland for temporary repairs before making a dash for the Clyde to be repaired.

Her first year in service had certainly been busy and eventful; she had more than proved her worth. She had steamed some 25,000 miles, chiefly in Atlantic convoys, and had never let a ship be lost through enemy action. On one occasion she had rescued an 8,000-ton American freighter carrying valuable army stores and armaments.

The ship, abandoned, sinking by the head and shipping water over the foredeck, was brought safely to Scotland by *Growler*. The freighter was repaired and by an interesting coincidence sailed twice afterwards in convoy with *Growler*.

Early in 1944 *Growler* returned to Campbeltown; with her repairs now completed she was ready for sea once more, so she sailed to rendezvous at Moville to join up with the outward-bound convoy to St Johns, Newfoundland. *Growler* returned to Campbeltown in March.

Fig 46 HMS *Growler* in wartime, with deck gun for'ard (image from Historical RFA).

In April 1944 she was responsible for towing the obsolete French battleship *Courbet* to Devonport for conversion into a breakwater for the proposed Allied invasion of France on the Normandy beaches. On 7 June, the day after the invasion began, *Growler* sailed from Weymouth with one of her sister ships, HMS *Samsonia*, towing *Courbet* across the English Channel to be sunk as part of the breakwater within which the Mulberry harbour would be built. Once *Courbet* had been scuttled successfully, *Growler* sailed back to England with the captain and skeleton crew of the old battleship.

(For more on the tow of *Courbet* to France to form some of the Gooseberry breakwaters at Sword Beach on D-Day, see Chapter 5.)

D-DAY – OPERATION PLUTO

Growler was also one of the tugs which, along with her sister ship *Bustler*, took part in Operation Pluto just after D-Day, to supply the invading armies with enough fuel to take the fight across northern France to Germany. The invasion was the biggest story of the war in Europe, and its importance cannot be over-emphasised, so I continue with some more background to the momentous occasion.

Along with the Mulberry harbours that were constructed immediately after D-Day, Operation Pluto is considered one of history's greatest feats of military engineering. The pipelines are also the forerunners of all flexible pipes used in the development of offshore oil fields.

Growler and *Bustler*, along with another smaller tug, towed the drums around 72 miles, and they were escorted by two Flower class corvettes, one of which, HMS *Dianthus*, happened to be another ship built in the Leith shipyards of Henry Robb.

Growler sailed on 19 June from Portsmouth in a convoy to Southend, arriving the next day, then sailed from Seine Bay in Convoy FTC 49 back to Southend.

In December 1944 she was tasked with towing the huge Admiralty Floating Dock (AFD 38) along with a compressor barge from Great Yarmouth to Harwich.

Fig 47 HMS *Dianthus*, Ship No 307 from the Henry Robb Shipyard (image from my own collection).

Fig 48 This photo gives some idea of the scale of the Conundrums; this one, having slipped its tow, had been washed up on the French coast. (Image is from the German website Operation Pluto, wlb-stuttgart.de.)

Two days after Christmas 1944 the powerful tug was dispatched to assist the tugs *Empire Jane* and *Empire Silas* in towing the huge Norwegian whale factory ship *Ole Wegger* down the River Seine. They were under strict orders to make sure that nothing untoward happened with the tow, and the local authorities also had orders to ensure that nothing got in the way. It was acknowledged that any mishap with the tow could close the Port of Rouen for an indefinite period, with the anticipated bad effect on the war effort.

The following is taken from the old book produced by the Henry Robb Shipyard not long after the war's end.

GROWLER

Another of the big tugs, HMS *Growler*, was, with her sister *Samsonia*, well to the fore in the landings in Normandy. They towed over large hulks and moored them into position off-shore to provide jetties behind which our ships could discharge their cargoes on the beaches. Both tugs lay off-shore doing all kinds of helpful jobs for the invasion armada for some days. At one period *Growler*'s guns were in action the whole night, but there were no casualties and no damage. Returning for their next trip, *Growler* and *Bustler* brought back some of the first of the wounded.

One incident shows the character of the men who man these ships. *Growler* was assisting a trawler which had been badly damaged by submerged ice in an eighty mile-an-hour gale. The donkey-man sent to man the pumps of the trawler was washed overboard into the raging, ice-cold sea, and by a miracle was washed back on board. He went quickly on pumping, told no one, even after he had been returned to the *Growler*, and no one would have known had not the Commander of the trawler reported the incident.

On 1 November 1944 *Growler* was in the southern reaches of the North Sea, off Westkapelle on Walcheren island, with the Bombardment Squadron,

Fig 49 George Caldwell Wilson, who served some time on HMRT *Growler* during the dark days of World War II. (Photo sent to me by Wilson's grandson, and reproduced here with his permission.)

Warspite, *Erebus* and *Roberts*. By January she was part of Convoy ATM 44 that left Antwerp en route to Southend, where she docked on 25 January 1945.

Growler was part of Force 135 for Operation Nestegg, to retake the Channel Islands. This was in May 1945, and the islands had been under German occupation since 1940 – the only part of the British Empire, as it was at the time, to be under German rule.

Towards the end of May *Growler* sailed from Liverpool in Convoy OS 130 KM, and until it dispersed the following day she was joined by HMRT *Reward*, another Leith-built tug. *Growler* was now destined for warmer waters in the Far East, as the Allies prepared to invade Japan. *Growler* was to join the British Pacific Fleet under the pennant number B 743, and it would be some years before she would see home waters again.

AFTER THE WAR

Fortunately, the Japanese surrendered before a full-scale invasion was unleashed on them, with the unthinkable numbers of extra casualties this might well have caused. The Japanese surrendered unconditionally on 2 September 1945.

Following the end of the war *Growler* was still in the Far East, and she was tasked with towing surrendered Japanese submarines. One of her jobs was to dispose of an ex-German U-boat operated by the Japanese as 107, towing to the Malacca Strait to be sunk.

Growler, now based at Singapore, was chartered in April 1947 to Moller Towages Ltd, Shanghai. With this her name was changed to *Caroline Moller*. The ending of the war did not mean that the big tugs would be in any less demand, as they were well suited to deep sea salvage and rescue operations, and were used extensively in them; the sea never takes a rest.

For the next couple of years as *Caroline Moller* she was kept busy with towing and salvage work such as helping to pull the 4,000-ton Shell Oil tanker *Cyrena* off a reef in New Guinea, and then, based at Fremantle in Australia, towing the fire-damaged SS *Cecil G. Sellars* to Singapore, then on to Hong Kong – all this after her engines had been repaired; just nine days before Christmas 1948, she had put into Champion Bay, Western Australia, anchoring just off Geraldton for repairs to her engines.

This was still a dangerous part of the world, as the *Canberra Times* of 2 July reported:

> The tug *Caroline Moller* was then sent to rescue the crew of the SS *Inchmark* which had run aground in the Arafura Sea north of Australia in June of 1949. The ship was a total loss and the tug arrived at Hong Kong on 1st July with all 38 of the crew safe.

Then on 21 July 1949 safe conduct was given by the Nationalist Chinese Government for *Caroline Moller* to go into Shanghai to tow the bomb-damaged Blue Funnel steamer *Anchises* to Kobe, Japan, for repairs. On the 29th *Caroline Moller* sailed from Shanghai with *Anchises* in tow, heading for Kobe and arriving there on 4 August.

No Christmas break for *Caroline Moller*, as she was called in to assist the Pan-American ship *Islas Visayas* bound for Amoy, China. The tug left Hong Kong on 26 December on hearing the *Islas Visayas* reporting that she had been boarded by pirates. Fortunately, by the time the ships had got to them the pirates had gone.

In January 1952 she took in tow the British freighter *Admiral Chase* between Colombo and Sumatra. The ship was being towed to Hong Kong for engine repairs.

Caroline Moller was then re-chartered to Hong Kong Salvage & Towing Co. Ltd, with another name change, this time *Castle Peak*. The big tug was soon earning her money when one of her first jobs was to sail from Hong Kong on 11 August 1952 to salvage the freighter *Plymouth Star* which had run aground off Wenchow (now Wenzhou), China.

The next note of interest in *Castle Peak* was when she called into Sydney from Formosa (now Taiwan) in February 1953. She was there to pick up the tow of not one but two ships: SS *Dilga* and SS *Dundula*, going to the breakers in Japan. This voyage began on 27 February, and the three vessels reached Yokohama on 6 April.

In November of the following year *Castle Peak* towed the British-registered freighter *Tefkros*, with a broken rudder, from the Formosa Strait to Hong Kong.

With her charter ended in the Far East in 1954 she returned to the Admiralty, to be re-renamed HMS *Growler* (pennant A 111). She was then transferred to the Royal Fleet Auxiliary (RFA) in 1957. She was back to normal peacetime duties, now with the prefix RFA, towing ships and floating docks around the British coast.

Although she was now back in home waters, the Admiralty had other plans for her as she was very much in demand for the charter towing business; so in 1958 she was chartered out once more to the very well-known towing company of United Towing Co. Ltd, Hull, who would rename her yet again, as *Welshman*. She was on a standard five-year charter to United Towing, to be returned to the Admiralty in 1963.

Interestingly some of her towing work was carried out for the Admiralty while under charter to United Towing, including towing the battleship HMS *Howe* to the shipbreaker's yard at Inverkeithing in June 1958. Her twin diesel power was required when the heavy and unwieldy battleship ran aground while they were approaching the yard; the entrance to Inverkeithing is well known as a difficult approach.

Later, *Growler*, or *Welshman* as she was now known, was involved in a collision with the paddle tug *Grinder* still in use at Portsmouth. Then the next November would see her back in the Far East, as she arrived at Hong Kong with USS *Shamrock Bay* in tow, heading for the ship breakers there.

The following two years would see a couple of unfortunate tragedies hit the ship, the first just two days after she had docked at Hong Kong with USS *Shamrock Bay*; the *Birmingham*

Post reported on 21 November 1959 that George Metcalfe, a 39-year-old seaman from Hull, had died following a fight on board *Welshman* the previous day. Then on the last day of August 1961 it was reported that Captain Ernest Bond, tug master of *Welshman*, had collapsed on the bridge and died while the vessel was on passage from Canada to Genoa.

From early December 1961 *Welshman* was assigned to tow a 2,800-ton mobile oil platform *Admar Constructor* from the Swan Hunter yard on the Tyne, where it had recently been constructed, and it was being delivered to the Middle East, but by 4 January 1962 the tug had lost the tow in heavy weather off the coast of Spain. The tow was reconnected as the weather calmed down a little, and *Welshman* and her charge continued to their destination.

Then on 23 October 1963 she returned to Admiralty service at Devonport, renamed *Cyclone* (still with pennant A 111).

A great deal of the ship's time was taken up towing obsolete Royal Navy ships and submarines from their home bases to the breakers' yards, primarily in Scotland. The Royal Navy was downsizing, it could be said, going from a world naval sea power to a much smaller navy, especially with the rapid technical advances that were making the older ships obsolete.

An interesting tow involved a couple of submarines, and this was also reported in *The Times* newspaper.

> It was December 1965 and *Cyclone* was towing two of her Majesty's submarines to Briton Ferry in Wales for demolition. She had HMS *Sea Scout* and HMS *Seraph* in tow. Two days later, on the 16th of December, the tow parted from HMS *Seraph*. A Naval Helicopter was dispatched to look for the submarine along with HMS *Hecla*; after 24 hours of searching she was at last spotted drifting towards Land's End. A naval crew were flown to the submarine to re-attach the tow to the tug *Cyclone*. It was the 10th of February 1966 before the submarine reached the breaker's yard in Wales.

Chief Officer John Hargreaves, who was there, tells a slightly different story: while they never saw *Hecla*, *Seraph* was never out of sight, so she was not in fact lost as reported at the time; see John's story in full further on in this chapter.

HMS *Seraph* (pennant number: P 219), an S class submarine, had been involved in much secret activity during World War II, hence the interest in the British press. She had been built for the Royal Navy, and had been completed in 1942 by Vickers Armstrong at Barrow-in-Furness. During the war she carried out multiple intelligence and special operations activities, the most notable of which was Operation Mincemeat.

After a much-needed overhaul in early 1943 HMS *Seraph* was ready for sea once more; her captain had just been briefed at the Admiralty about Operation Mincemeat. This would be carried out by the submarine upon her return to the Mediterranean. This top-secret mission was part of the plan, codenamed Operation Barclay, to convince the Germans

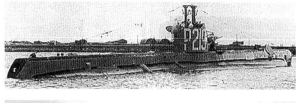

Left: Fig 50 HMS *Seraph*, S class submarine (image from the Barrow-in-Furness Submariners, Association, shown on Wikipedia, Operation Mincemeat).

Middle: Fig 51 *Cyclone*, ex-*Growler* (image by Michael Williams on rfanostalgia, shown by kind permission).

Lower: Fig 52 *Growler* after her return to the British Admiralty and renamed *Cyclone*, A111. Photo from RFAA plymouth.

that the Allies intended to land their forces in Greece and on Sardinia, and not, as secretly planned, on Sicily. For more about this operation, read on.

The tow of HMS *Seraph* is told by John Hargreaves, who was on *Cyclone* at the time. I am indebted to him for giving me permission to reproduce the story, which was posted on the RFANostalgia.net website in 2018. The ten images below are all from John Hargreaves, with his permission to use in this book.

RFA *Cyclone* and Submarine *Seraph*

Chief Officer John Hargreaves shares his story:

The crew of RFA CYCLONE, a big Bustler class ocean-going tug, was looking forward to a Xmas in our home port of Portsmouth and we had just completed putting up our Xmas decorations in the wardroom when we got orders to take the submarine HMS SERAPH to a lay-up berth at Swansea in the Bristol Channel. It was mid-December 1965, which would give us nice time to do the job before Xmas. The weather forecast for the next couple of weeks was lousy, but CYCLONE was then one of the biggest tugs in the world. Initially known as HMT GROWLER she was built by Henry Robb of Leith and, after the war had various names under commercial companies before returning to the Admiralty as RFA CYCLONE in 1963 and being completely refitted at Portsmouth.

HMS SERAPH was the last of the S-class submarines and had been decommissioned since 1962 and was now due to be scrapped. She had distinguished herself during the war by carrying Lt. Gen. Mark Clark to North Africa for secret negotiations with Vichy French officers before the Torch landings and then again by secretly taking aboard French General Henri Giraud for a meeting with General Eisenhower in Gibraltar. Because Giraud flatly refused to deal with the British, and there was no US boat within 3,000 miles, HMS SERAPH briefly became the "USS SERAPH", flying the US Navy ensign and becoming "the ship with two captains" for Operation Kingpin.

After a refit at Blyth, SERAPH sailed again in April 1943, carrying a special passenger. This was a corpse in a metal canister, packed in dry ice, and dressed in a Royal Marines uniform. Attached to the corpse was a briefcase containing faked "secret documents" designed to mislead the Axis. In the early hours of 30 April SERAPH surfaced off the coast of Spain and launched the body and briefcase in the water. SERAPH then radioed the signal "MINCEMEAT completed" while continuing to Gibraltar. The body was picked up by the Spanish, who decided it was a courier killed in an aircraft accident. The false documents were passed to the Germans and led them to divert forces from the defence of Sicily.

SERAPH remained in active service after the war and was streamlined by reducing the size of the conning tower, removing the gun along with one of the periscopes and the radar mast, and the torpedo tubes were blanked over. In 1955 she was fitted with armour plating and used as a torpedo target boat. Her number was changed to P219 to S89, presumably because of NATO.

I was the Chief Officer of CYCLONE and I went aboard SERAPH with a working party to make an inspection as usual to ensure that everything that was supposed to be closed was shut and that nothing had been left unsecured. The hatches had been closed and welded by the dockyard and a length of chain had been secured to her forward bitts which terminated just forward of the bullring. We shackled a 5-fathom towing pennant of 5" wire

Fig 53 Choff John Hargreaves.

to this and flaked it out on the forward casing and we mounted battery powered navigation lights on the conning tower which would be turned on by the harbour tug crew when they delivered the submarine to us. We got approval to sail next morning at 0800 hours.

RFA CYCLONE got under way next morning, moved out into the centre of the harbour and SERAPH was brought to our stern by a harbour tug about 0900 hours. The dockyard crew lowered the end of the 5" pennant to us, we shackled our main 5" towing wire to this, the harbour tug turned on the submarine's lights, cast off and we were on our way. The weather was lousy – cold and raining with the wind about force 4 to 5 – but the submarine followed very nicely on a short towline until we got clear of the harbour entrance. CYCLONE's main towing wire was a 5" flexible steel wire rope, 350 fathoms long and weighing about 5 tonnes, kept on an automatic winch which could be adjusted for whatever pull we required. Once clear of the harbour, we paid out about 50 metres but SERAPH stayed nicely behind us until we cleared the Needles and got into the open sea when we went to our normal towing length of 200 fathoms and increased speed to about 7 knots. It's very important, on an ocean tow, to keep some 'spring' in the tow wire to allow for the massive weights of the tug and her tow and this is done by allowing the weight of the wire itself to form a catenary between the stern of the tug and the bow of the tow.

The 5" tow wire has breaking strength of about 100 tonnes and CYCLONE's automatic winch was rated at 40 tonnes. SERAPH was towing at about 10 to 12 tonnes. The weather remained unpleasant, and we were pitching heavily with spray flying everywhere. SERAPH was taking seas from one end to the other but, as a submarine with absolutely nothing on her casing, there was nothing to get carried away and she seemed to be towing easily enough. As is almost always the case, with a vessel under tow, she 'sailed' to windward a bit and lay about 20 degrees on our starboard quarter. We seemed to have the ocean to ourselves and made some jokes about everyone (but us) staying in port for Xmas. Soon after dark the green sidelight on SERAPH went out (or was carried away) but we could still see where she was by the spray and broken water and we took an occasional look at her by searchlight. She was fine and by midnight on December 14th we were passing Start Point.

The weather worsened, with the wind increasing to a full gale from the southwest and driving rain most of the time. On the afternoon of Tuesday the 15th we had rounded Land's End and the wind increased to storm force from the southwest but the forecast was for it to moderate by morning. We had to slow down and to avoid getting into more congested and shallower water the Captain decided to stay in the deeper water further offshore. SERAPH was lying wide on the port side and we shortened the tow wire to about 150 fathoms. Just after 2000 hours there was a hell of a bang and the automatic winch started heaving in – SERAPH was gone. We hauled in the tow wire and found that there was only about 100 fathoms of it and the last 50, or so, was heavily damaged. It had obviously struck an unmarked wreck and been severed.

We closed on SERAPH and examined her closely by searchlight. She seemed fine so we advised all shipping, and the Admiralty, of where we were and what had happened. SERAPH was lying head to wind and drifting fairly slowly, to some extent anchored by the tow wire dragging along the bottom. The next thing to arrive was

Fig 54 The second officer's photo of *Seraph* under tow by RFA *Cyclone* in awfully bad weather.

the Penlee (Land's End) lifeboat, the coxswain of which offered to put men aboard SERAPH but this would have been impractical – it's extremely difficult to board a submarine at sea because of the shape.

We did, however, accept the offer of close inspection of SERAPH so I and my Bosun went aboard the lifeboat, and we went and checked her over. We could see that the 5" pennant through the bullring looked undamaged but would have to be cut away as it would be impossible to recover it. The relative motion of the two vessels was considerable – one moment we were looking down on the submarine's bow and the next we were looking at her forefoot, probably at least a 10-to-12-foot difference. The lifeboat returned us to CYCLONE and that was an exciting incident as well but both of us made it undamaged. We were advised by radio that two helicopters from the Naval Air Station at Culdrose would arrive shortly after first light to assist us in the recovery if the weather conditions were suitable.

Next morning the wind had eased off although the forecast was not so good, but we decided to give it a try. Unfortunately, SERAPH had a jumper wire from the top of her periscope to both ends and therefore the only place to 'land' on her was at the aft end of the casing, clear of the jumper wire – a place about two feet wide by six or seven feet long. There was a lifeline, at about waist height, on both the fore and aft casings but nothing around the conning tower. I was young and fit in those days and felt quite confident that I could make it OK and my Bosun and a couple of big, tough, sailors volunteered to give it a go. We figured that, at the worst, we'd go in the water but the second helicopter was right there to scoop anyone up pretty quickly before the cold could do us much harm. Just by coincidence, the helicopter that lifted us was number 89, the same number as SERAPH.

I was picked up by the helicopter and, in a minute or so, was dangling over the submarine's casing which was rising and falling a couple of metres every few seconds as she pitched. She was also rolling a bit but the helicopter pilot

Left: Fig 55 Chopper lifting from *Cyclone.*

Middle: Fig 56 *Seraph*'s small conning tower was useless for landing on by the 'boarding party', and it was exceedingly difficult for the men to move forward and aft.

Lower: Fig 57 Last of the boarding team lowered onto *Seraph.*

Fig 58 Chopper departing after landing the last man.

was very good even though it was still blowing pretty hard. I pushed the safety grommet up so that I could very quickly get clear of the strop by just lifting my arms up when my feet touched the casing and I figured that I'd be able to grab the stanchion at the aft end of the lifeline before I lost my balance.

This worked like a charm – the pilot brought me across SERAPH's stern at just the right height, the casing came up under my feet and without even thinking about it I threw my arms up and was clear of the strop and grabbing for the stanchion. The one thing I was not expecting (stupidly) was the slipperiness of the casing and I want down pretty heavily but managed to keep a deathly grip on the stanchion and quickly get back to my feet. I hitched myself to the stanchion so as to have both arms free.

My Bosun, Jock Topp, was the next across and I was able to grab him and keep his balance until he also hitched his lifeline to the stanchion. Then came the two seamen, Penson and Bend, who hitched themselves to the lifeline and moved forward whilst the helicopter made several more trips, bringing the gear we reckoned we needed.

We then had to move the gear, and a bag of water and sandwiches, to the forward casing and this wasn't so easy because the submarine was rolling and the casing was wet. We had quite a bit of spray coming over us and it was cold.

The end of the casing, near the bow, was very narrow, and occasionally dipped almost under water as she pitched. CYCLONE came very close, someone threw a heaving line across, and we hauled a messenger line over, followed by a short 3½" wire pennant and a couple of shackles, and we lashed the pennant to the sonar domes on the forward casing for the time being. There were some little toe-holes in the sides of the casing which ensured that we got thoroughly soaked. With a lot of difficulty, we managed to unscrew the shackle between the chain through the bullring and drop the broken tow wire. That should have been a very quick job but it seemed to take forever because of the position of the shackle, the fairly violent motion of the bow and the occasional sea coming up but, eventually, with a great deal of prying and hammering, the shackle pin moved enough to clear the chain and the tow line fell away.

We were all wet and very cold by then and, at about this time, I suddenly remembered that it was my wedding anniversary and would really rather have been doing something else at this time. I remember making some comment about this to the other guys and that they seemed to think it was very funny.

The weather was rapidly getting worse, with the wind backing around to the northwest, we had the north Cornish coast to leeward. With the drag of the towline gone the submarine lay beam on to the seas and the rolling became much worse with a fair amount of spray coming over us.

It was impossible to stand on the casing without a firm grip on the lifeline so, mostly, we had to sort of crawl around. If it was possible to get any wetter, we did. Whilst we were doing this, Arthur Briggs, the Second Bosun, and the other seamen had got a 100-fathom length of 3½" wire rope out of CYCLONE's hold and flaked it out on the towing deck with stoppers attached so that it could be controlled as it ran out.

Once we had got rid of the tow wire, it was straightforward. We shackled the pennant to the chain through the bullring and CYCLONE came awfully close again – Captain Murray was a very good ship handler, probably the best I ever sailed with – and passed us the end of the 3½" emergency tow wire and we shackled the two wires together. We cut the rope and that was that – SERAPH was under tow again although only on a 3½" wire which meant that we had to take it very easy. The one thing we all completely forgot, and which we could very easily have done whilst CYCLONE was so close, was to get something like hot soup or whatever, hauled across. Too late now, as CYCLONE was several hundred feet away and we'd eaten all the sandwiches long ago.

With SERAPH again under tow, even very slowly, she 'sailed' up windward as usual and now had a nasty pitching motion as well. Quite unpleasant – see the photo the Second Officer took. The wind was by now getting pretty strong and it was considered too dangerous to try to get us off the tiny little stern where we 'landed' but we had to get off somehow. The conning tower was very small and there was really no shelter anywhere as the spray was coming over continuously. We were all tired, soaked and really, really cold, and we lashed ourselves to the two sonar domes. Our hands were so cold that it was a bit difficult to make our fingers work properly and I was very concerned that one of us would get adrift, in which case he'd be lost for sure. Darkness was coming quite quickly.

CYCLONE launched her Zodiac inflatable, and Arthur Briggs came to get us. The shape of the submarine, with her curved side tanks, meant that we each in turn had to jump from the bow as the boat came up on a swell and, in the dark, the chances of us being recovered if we went into the water were not too good.

This was actually the most dangerous part of the whole operation, but we all made it OK, with nothing worse than a few more bruises, and we were soon safely back aboard CYCLONE. We got to Swansea next day.

About a month later after reading the Captain's report of the voyage, the C-in-C Portsmouth said our efforts were 'commendable'.

When I spoke to my wife by phone, she told me that she'd switched on the radio for the 8 AM news and there we were – headline news, but they just reported that the tow had parted, and we were recovering it.

In March 1966 *Cyclone* sailed from Portsmouth with HMS *Berry Head* in tow for Devonport, then in July it was back to the Middle East to tow HMS *Kedeston* back to Devonport. Then it was back to towing submarines going to the breakers as she towed

Above: Fig 59 *Seraph* delivered to the breaker's yard, *Cyclone* in the background.

Right: Fig 60 Commendation from C-in-C Portsmouth.

R.F.A. CYCLONE   24-1-66

The following is an extract from a letter received from C-in-C, Portsmouth:-

1.   I have read the report of your tow of HMS SERAPH to Swansea on 14th to 17th December and have noted the difficulties that you encountered when the tow parted.

2.   The manner in which you and your ~~crew~~ ship's company recovered the tow in spite of worsening weather conditions is commendable, the efforts of the following men being particularly praiseworthy:

            Chief Officer J, Hargreaves
            Beatswain J. Topp
            Second Beatswain A. Briggs
            Able Seaman R. Penson
            Able Seaman R. Bond

            Signed V.C. BEGG
            Admiral
            Commander-in-Chief
            21-1-66

            ....
            Master
            RFA CYCLONE

SECRET SERVICE SHIP'S LAST VOYAGE

FROM OUR NAVAL CORRESPONDENT

The Navy's S class submarine H.M.S. Seraph, the centre of much secret activity in the Second World War, has made an adventurous last journey to the breakers' yard in Swansea. The submarine broke away while under tow down the English Channel, and spent 24 hours drifting helplessly off Land's End.

The Navy's hydrographic ship Hecla had searched for her and a Wessex helicopter from Culdrose circled the Channel. When the Seraph was sighted three men were transferred from the tug Cyclone to the submarine to restore the towline.

Fig 61 The newspaper cutting; although the account was less than accurate, it was *The Times* that reported it.

HMS *Solebay* to Troon, on the Ayrshire coast of the Firth of Clyde, arriving on 11 August 1967. *Cyclone* then sailed back down to Devonport to pick up HMS *Ursa* for demolition in Newport, Wales.

In 1971 *Cyclone* was transferred to the Royal Maritime Auxiliary Service (RMAS). The following is from Wikipedia, giving some background on the RMAS:

The Royal Maritime Auxiliary Service (RMAS) had merged with the former Port Auxiliary Service (PAS) in 1976 to form a component of Her Majesty's Naval Service that was known as marine services. Marine services existed to support the operations of the Royal Navy, Royal Marines and Royal Fleet Auxiliary.

In April 1973 *Cyclone* towed *Arquina*, which had been severely damaged by fire, into Tenerife for examination.

But then in 1977 *Cyclone* was laid up at Gibraltar, and five years later she was put on the disposal list, now surplus to the Royal Navy's requirements.

In April 1983 she was sold to Eagle Tugs Ltd, to be based at Mombasa and registered in Grand Cayman under the new name *Martial*.

Left: Fig 62 *Growler*'s badge (image from Historical RFA).

Lower left: Fig 63 RFA *Growler* (photo from Historical RFA).

Lower right: Fig 64 Tug *Martial*, formerly RFA *Growler*, alongside at Mombasa (photo © Kevin Patience, published with his consent).

It was on 21 January 1985 when this fine old ship took her last voyage, sailing from Djibouti and across the Indian Ocean once more, but this time to be broken up for scrap. She arrived at the ship graveyard on Gadani Beach, Karachi, on 30 January 1985.

From her launch at Leith in September 1942 to her final resting place on the beach at Karachi, *Growler* must have travelled many thousands of miles through the perils of wartime U-boats to surviving some of the worst weather on the planet, saving many ships and men.

The following are some comments that were sent into my old website and blog on Leith-built ships from ex-crew and interested people, reproduced here unabridged.

Brian Tomlinson

I served on the *Welshman (Growler)* as a cabin boy. Then on station at Falmouth. She had an inscription written on a panel in the port side alleyway that read "Boston to Hong Kong". We were towing a Great Lakes cargo boat from Quebec to Genoa when the captain passed away. He was Captain Bond who had been involved in towing the Mulberry harbours during WW2. The navigating officer was a Captain Chinery. I have great memories of an unforgettable experience.

In reply to Brian's comment shown above:

Iain Wilson

I have been doing a bit of reading on the web (I also bought a dvd about the tug boats) about the rescue tugs. It is a pity that during wartime there was an embargo on photographing and filming on them. I have found bits and pieces about them but information is scarce.

I know that my Grandad served on her from August 1942 until the end of the war and would have been aboard when they were towing the Mulberry harbours into place.

From what I have read and heard these were a group of servicemen who were extremely brave and served under extreme conditions (like most others).

I know my grandad was severely affected and never slept in a dark room after the war

John Pinkerton

My Great Uncle, Victor Williamson, from Portadown Co Armagh, was the radio officer on HMS *Growler* during WW2. My brother has his diaries and a few bits and pieces which might be of interest.

James Sandison

My father James Andrew Sandison, along with his friend Andrew William Wishart – both from Shetland Isles – served on *Growler* for most of the war.

The men who served on the big tugs did not mince their words, and I like this brief description from John Hargreaves, when he tells me of his first impressions of the tug, at the time named *Growler*, as follows:

She'd been on charter 'out East' with, I think, a Chinese crew. The ship was lying at a buoy and was deserted, all the previous crew long gone. Dicky Dawes, the Chief Engineer and I, went aboard by boat and we entered the starboard alleyway with flashlights, the ship had no power. I suddenly stopped, the Chief banging into me, because I caught a glimpse of pale sunlight where there should have been darkness – coming through the sheer strake just under the seamen's washroom sinks. We looked, with flashlights, and saw that, indeed, the sheer strake had corroded right through.

We went on with a cursory inspection after getting a generator started and found that the ship was very badly in need of a major refit. I signed on a crew and went through the process of registering her as an RFA and changing her name to CYCLONE. One of the first jobs for the new crew was to physically paint the new name on bow and stern and, after that, we did a complete stock-take of the hold and storerooms and spent a number of days preparing a defect list. All accommodation spaces were stripped out, whether by the previous crew or others, I don't know. Bedding, furniture, all gone.

She was, indeed, a decrepit old wreck. Apart from the daylight streaming through the hull where it should not have been, the wheelhouse windows must have been leaking badly for years as the deck plating had corroded right through. Actual holes and the deck plates were slightly springy underfoot.

The Chief and I had a couple of meetings with Admiralty representatives, and it was determined that she would go to Portsmouth for a refit. I forget the actual length of time it took to repair the damage, but she was a completely different vessel when finished. One thing about her, that I left in (the Admiralty didn't want to change it) was the rather silly giant roller at the stern. Silly because the tow wire will, inevitably, lie against the gog post on one side or the other and will never pass over the roller except when going from one side to the other.

HMRT *HESPERIA*

The keel for the next in line of the Bustler class was laid down at Leith on 25 March 1942, two months after the keel for *Growler* had been laid down. The new tug would be Ship No 329 in the Henry Robb Shipyard's order book.

She had the same eight months on the slipway being built and she was launched on 10 November 1942; Mrs C.C. Walcott would name her HMRT *Hesperia*.

With a five-month fitting-out period followed by successful sea trials she was accepted by the Royal Navy and commissioned on 9th February 1943.

She was the fourth in line of the much-needed large deep sea rescue tugs to be built at the yard – a yard that was working flat out, along with all the other shipyards around Britain, as they entered the fourth year of war.

Hesperia entered service on the dangerous Atlantic convoy route, and she was responsible for the salvaging of some 15 ships damaged by the enemy, while in her first year in service she steamed some 38,237 miles.

For a brand-new vessel this was tough going, but *Hesperia* came through, proving the justification, if any was needed, of her proud builders.

Early October 1943 *Hesperia* was assigned as a rescue tug to one of the slow-moving convoys going through the Mediterranean. They would form up at Gibraltar and voyage on through the Med, with ships peeling off from the 100-ship convoy as they neared the intended destination. As well as the threat from Italian submarines (and later, U-boats) the convoys had to contend with air attacks by German and Italian aircraft. The Italian navy also presented a formidable barrier to the movement of ships in the area.

Hesperia was attached to Convoy KMS 28, joining from Malta and reaching Alexandria with 16 ships in total, before going on to Port Said.

She was to spend most of her time in the Mediterranean, and this would be where she would meet her eventual fate. She was assigned to a tow along with another tug, *Empire Sandy*, tasked with taking the Admiralty Floating Dock (ADF 24) to Port Said. A huge storm hit the area on 8 February 1945 with wind speeds recorded above 100 mph. *Hesperia* battled the elements, along with the smaller, less powerful, *Empire Sandy*. When the hawser of *Empire Sandy* parted, in such conditions reconnection was impossible. As *Hesperia* desperately hung onto her tow, a huge floating dock swinging around madly, her master intended to try and ride out the gale. But the wind was onshore and so fierce that the dock, presenting a formidable wind surface, began to drift towards the rocks. In a desperate battle against nature the strain was just too much and the hawser connecting *Hesperia* to her charge parted. The commander, in a desperate effort to save his tow, put the tug up against the leeward side of the dock and tried to push it out to sea.

But even with both her engines at full power, producing more than 3,200 horsepower to her single shaft, she was no match for Mother Nature. The tug and the dock were driven ashore on a barren coast, and both were so severely damaged that they were lost. Such was the damage inflicted by the storm on *Hesperia* that she was declared a total constructive

Fig 65 *Empire Sandy* cruising the Great Lakes of Canada. What a wonderful way to restore an old ship! (Image from Paul Chaplin.)

loss, past repair. To have survived the worst that the enemy could throw at her, this was an unfortunate and sad end to an exceptionally fine ship.

Amazingly, however, *Empire Sandy* is still going strong and is now a converted vessel with masts, doing adventure cruises out of Toronto around the Great Lakes.

Remarkably close in design to the Bustler class with the same elliptical stern, the old tugs did look very much like old-time schooners from midships aft, a pedigree running through the design of a lot of old ships: if it looks good then in general it is good. *Hesperia* was the only one of the Leith-built tugs lost during World War II – and that was down to the weather, not the enemy.

> The *Empire Sandy*'s website lists her World War II official log books. The entry in logbook TNA-25-5-05-94 is from 8 February 1945, when she was towing, in company with *Hesperia*, ADF24, and had to slip her towline due to the storm, after which *Hesperia* and ADF24 were blown ashore on the coast of Libya and were lost.

The following is a comment sent into my old website and blog on Leith-built ships, reproduced here unabridged.

Paul Chaplin

The *Empire Sandy*'s website lists her World War II official log books. The entry in logbook TNA-25-5-05-94 is from 8 February 1945, when she was towing, in company with *Hesperia*, ADF24, and had to slip her towline due to the storm, after which *Hesperia* and ADF24 were blown ashore on the coast of Libya and were lost.

7: *MEDIATOR*

The keels for the next two Bustler class tugs would go down in late 1943, with the build anticipated to take the same eight months; the first in line was launched on 21 June 1944.

As she was readied on the slipway, just as the shipwrights hammered out the daggers Mrs Peter Fraser named Ship No 335 HMS *Mediator*.

With a five-month fitting-out period followed by successful sea trials she was accepted by the Royal Navy and commissioned on 8 November 1944.

Although she was too late for D-Day there was still a war going on worldwide, and *Mediator* was to go straight from the Henry Robb Shipyard on a voyage of 14,000 miles' continuous steaming. Of this distance 6,000 miles included heavy towing, the longest of 3,700 miles non-stop at an average speed of 7 knots. As the yard said, this was a severe trial for a new ship – a trial that *Mediator* passed with flying colours.

There would be more voyages over the Atlantic for *Mediator*, as she was used in the towing of Admiralty Floating Docks (AFD), fabricated in America for use in Europe and the UK.

The large tugs of the Bustler class were used in tandem to tow anything that floated at the time to anywhere the tow might be required. *Mediator*, along with *Samsonia*, was used to tow AFD 31 from New York to Gibraltar, then the two tugs returned for another trip. This time tasked with towing ADF 32, and for this tow there would be three tugs involved with *Envoy* (later RFA *Envoy*) and *Samsonia* towing over the wide Atlantic from America via San Juan, Puerto Rico, to Oran, to be met by *Mediator* for the passage eastwards through Gibraltar Strait. They passed through the strait on 11 April 1945, arriving in Oran on 13 April.

A floating dock is a type of pontoon where you can dry-dock vessels; the dock has floodable tanks, just as a submarine has, with stability achieved by the careful use of flooding and emptying the tanks. With a large double bottom, the dock has two walls forming a U-section whose huge side walls provide stability once the bottom section is flooded. Valves are used to flood and empty the tanks; when the valves are opened the tanks fill with water taking the dock floor under the surface of the sea, which then allows a

Fig 66 *Mediator* (photo from RFAnostalgia.org).

Fig 67 Admiralty Floating Dock No 1, built in 1900 by Swan Hunter on the Tyne to a design by Clark & Standfield. It was a floating graving dock and had a lift of 16,500 tons. (Image from my own collection.)

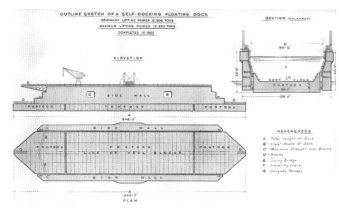

waiting vessel to be manoeuvred between the walls of the dock. The tanks are then blown using high pressure air, making the structure, along with the vessel aboard it, rise above the surface of the sea. Then whatever repair work is necessary can be carried out.

The larger floating dry docks consisted of a number of sections which could be combined to handle ships of various lengths. Each section contained its own equipment for emptying the tanks and to provide services. The AFDs were of different sizes and were never given names, just a number following the prefix AFD. The largest of the AFDs could dock the Royal Navy's biggest vessels.

Another advantage of the floating dry docks was that they could be moved to wherever they were needed during World War II. However, they were notoriously difficult to tow, with their large walls forming a huge sail area in high winds; some of the AFD tows could take months at an average speed of only 3–4 knots.

AFDs were used extensively all over the world; they were crucial to the Royal Navy as not all ships, in the event of mishap or enemy action, could reach a suitable port with conventional dry docks.

Left: Fig 68 Clive's diary shows the date when he was called to serve on *Mediator* during his national service as stoker/mechanic 1st class 1949–1950. (Image from Clive Reynolds.)

Right: Fig 69 The crew of *Mediator* taken in 1949 (photograph sent to me by Clive Reynolds and reproduced with his permission).

Mediator was to spend most of her time in the Mediterranean, out of the huge Royal Navy base in Malta; from there she could reach any part of this area of sea in a relatively short time should the need arise.

She was a popular ship, and we have been sent a lot of information from some of the men who served on her; the following is from Clive Reynolds who was called up to her in 1949.

From 1956 she was Royal Navy-manned at Malta, and for two and a half years of this time she was commanded by Lieutenant Commander Peter Alexander Coryton Day. His son, Kenneth J.C. Day, Captain RN 1964–2009) was good enough to send me the story of his father's time with HMS *Mediator*, from which the following is extracted; this is a fine first-hand account of what it was like to command one of the large Bustler class tugs. (NB The images accompanying this story, from Fig 70 to Fig 90, are from the memoirs of Lieutenant Commander Peter Day, kindly loaned to me by his son, Captain K.J.C. Day, and reproduced by his permission.)

H.M.S. MEDIATOR –1956–59

I had two years and six months, December 1956 to May 1959 as Commanding Officer of H.M.S. Mediator, a Bustler Class Ocean Rescue Tug, in the Mediterranean. Our complement was 5 officers, 4 RN senior rates, a signalman, a telegraphist and 40 Maltese crew.

I was delighted to hear from Colin Litster, whose grandfather served on HMS *Mediator* from 1944 to 1948.

Colin tells me the following story about another very special person, serving on a very special ship built at Leith. He has also kindly allowed the use of the following images from Lt Cdr Litster, showing his time on the rescue tug *Mediator*.

Lt Cdr Alexander
Litster, DSC

> My grandfather – Lt Cdr Alexander Litster – was on *Mediator* from December 1944 to late 1948. He joined her at Reykjavik, having been skipper of the Lend-Lease tug HMRT *Bold* for about two and a half years, mostly in the Indian Ocean. Before *Bold* he had been skipper of a few anti-submarine trawlers. He received the DSC for services in Norway and had also spent about two years in Iceland.

> Most of his wartime service on *Mediator* seemed to be based around the towing of a floating dock from the US to the Med. After this he returned to the UK just in time for VE Day.

> Post war I don't know much about. He was in various ports around the UK for a while. At the end of the war a number of the tug captains were invited to sign on for another five years as RN officers. I guess there was a lot of

HMS *Mediator* is the ship nearest the camera, leading the way while towing the centre section of *AFD 35*. The floating dock had been built in Bombay and was the largest in the world at the time. It was in sections, to be joined at Malta. This operation was given the name Operation Snow White; the tow had an average speed of around 5 knots.

The large tugs position the Centre Section, as seen in this image above.

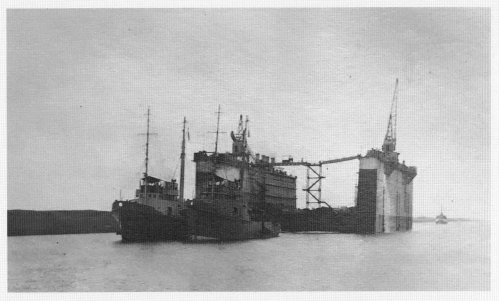

AFD 35 Centre Section moves slowly through the Suez Canal 1947.

tidying up to do! The highlight of course was the towing of *AFD 35* from Bombay to Malta in 1947.

He left *Mediator* to join *Marauder* (based in Malta), and stayed in the rescue tug service until 1952, when he left the navy.

HMS *Mediator* leads AFD 35 through the Suez Canal.

HMS *Vanguard* Gunnery Practise in May 1949.

HMS *Vanguard*'s shots straddle the target, being towed by HMS *Mediator*.

The crew of *Mediator* prepare the battle practise target for more punishment, before once more towing it out into the Mediterranean.

This was to be Local Foreign Service based on Malta, so [his wife and son] Betty and Colin were able to accompany me except that Betty and I flew out to Malta in separate aircraft. Ken unfortunately had to be left at boarding school but would fly out for the holidays.

This was at the time of the Suez Crisis and my ship *Mediator* was down at Port Said. I flew out to Malta on a Service flight, from there straight on to Cyprus without seeing Betty in Malta, and then on to Port Said to join *Mediator*. Betty and Colin flew out to Malta British European Airways, and although we landed very much at the same time, we were not able to meet. Fortunately, we had some particularly good friends at the RN Air Station at Halfar, Commander and Mrs R C (Bob and Gwyn) Allen, who put them both up while Betty searched for accommodation and Colin was enrolled at the junior Naval School.

We, the ship, were not delayed too long at Port Said and we returned to Malta when Betty and Colin were safely installed in a flat in Gunlayer Square, Floriana, near Valletta, on the top floor, 95 stairs from ground level with no lift, overlooking Grand Harbour where *Mediator* berthed. So life went on, very pleasantly despite the constant smell of the Floriana drains.

Our main job was towing Battle Practice Targets for the ships of the Mediterranean Fleet. On one occasion I had to haul down the Black Flag, which was the permission to fire, because the first salvo of 6-inch shells from a cruiser who shall be nameless were landing ahead of my towing ship, whereas the target was half a mile astern! On another occasion the US Battleship Iowa was firing at our target, again half a mile astern of us, with its 15-inch guns. This was very impressive because each turret produced a different coloured smoke from its guns, red, white, and blue.

It was very good shooting, so much so that not only was the target hit a number of times, but a shell must have severed the towing wire and suddenly the target was adrift. That was the end of the shooting for the day, but we had to recover the target. There was quite a sea running and I had to manoeuvre the *Mediator* stern first with a single screw up to the target so that one of my lads could jump from our stern down on to it. These Battle Practice Targets were about 30 feet long, extremely low in the water, very heavy and built with superstructure all made of wood and canvas so that they could be seen from a long distance away.

Fig 70 Betty and Peter Day with their son Ken, just off the plane at Luqa Airport, 1958.

We also did various long distance towing jobs, such as when the destroyer *Undaunted* – we called her the *Indented* – managed to run into the wooden minesweeper *Maxton* and came off worst herself. We had to tow the *Undaunted* stern first from Cyprus back to Malta over Christmas. She did pass over to us by heaving line a bottle of whiskey in part payment!

We also towed the *Manxman*, a Fast Minelayer, from Malta to Gibraltar – I mentioned her earlier in 1941, a Lifting Craft from Malta through the Suez Canal to Aden and a Search and Rescue Operation for a small Italian ship which sent out an SOS. This signal came through early in the morning and we sailed as soon as possible with all the officers onboard but only two thirds of the ship's company.

The Naval Provost Marshal kept a list of the addresses of all the officers and ship's company so that, providing they were at home at night, they could be contacted. Because we were the first to arrive in the reported position which was thirty miles south of Malta, we became Officer in Charge of the search, and we were later joined by two coastal minesweepers and the aircraft carrier *Centaur*.

We searched all day, including aircraft from the *Centaur*, and were about to give up for the night as it was getting dark, when my First Lieutenant thought he saw something in the distance. We immediately altered course to investigate and found it was a small boat with six occupants, one of whom had died shortly before.

We reported the discovery by signal to the Commander-in-Chief Mediterranean at Malta, took them onboard and returned to harbour at our best speed. The boat had been adrift having run out of fuel and was a long way from the reported position. The vessel had been overcome by the sea and the Captain and crew had taken to the one lifeboat. It was very satisfying to have rescued the crew but unfortunate that we didn't find them before the one man had died.

We had some incredibly happy times on board, a number of cocktail parties, boat trips to Comino and Gozo – small islands off Malta, escorting the Naval yacht race to Syracuse in Sicily and a Families Day trip round Malta. Oh, and I almost forgot, when Betty's mother flew out to Malta to stay with us for a few weeks, Betty and she went across to Syracuse in a small ship called the Star of Malta for a short visit. When she went home she took passage in a Royal Fleet Auxiliary called the *Amherst* and greatly enjoyed the voyage,

So, in May 1959, my time in *Mediator* came to an end and I handed over the ship to my successor, after two years and five months, on the jetty in Syracuse. Betty and I had decided to drive overland from Sicily back to UK by car. Colin had flown home to his aunt in England to start at a preparatory school, St Bede's in Eastbourne.

I had obtained permission from CinC Med's staff for Betty to take passage in *Mediator* to Syracuse so we hoisted our car onboard, our heavy luggage had already been crated up and dispatched by ship for home.

It was a most interesting trip home taking three weeks and calling in at Catania and Messina in Sicily, up the west coast of Italy via Amalfi, Vesuvius, Rome, Perugia, Florence, Bologna, Padua and Venice. Then over the Arlberg Pass into Switzerland and up to Lake Constance.

From there into Germany and Heidelberg, then down the Rhine to Mainz, Coblenz and Cologne, into Belgium and to Aachen, Bruges and finally Ostend for the crossing to Dover.

The above is an extract from a book which Captain Ken Day's father, Lieutenant Commander Peter Alexander Coryton Day wrote in 2003 about his life and times in the Royal Navy between 1938 and 1967.

Captain Ken Day added:

During that period Lieutenant Commander Peter Alexander Coryton Day served in the following ships:

HMS *Erebus* – 1938	HMS *Romola* – 1946–47
HMS *Vindictive* – 1938	HMS *Sluys* & HMS *Collingwood* – 1948–50
HMS *Cumberland* – 1939–40	HMS *Glory* – 1950–53
Sub Lieutenant's Courses – 1941	HMS *Daedalus* & HMS *Coll* – 1953–56
HMS *Cossack* – 1941	HMS *Mediator* -1956–59
HMS/M *Taku* – 1942–44	HMS *Vanguard* & CinC Plymouth Sea Cadet Corps – 1964–67
HMS *Nigeria* – 1944–46	

The following story is from an article in *The Times of Malta* from 23 March 1957, by *The Times* service reporter:

INCIDENT AT SEA

Fleet Tug *Mediator*'s Long Task

Her Majesty's Fleet Tug *Mediator*, Lieutenant Commander P.A.C. Day in command, left Grand Harbour recently on what was meant to be just another Battle Target Tow. It ended up by being quite a trip, with a charging disabled B.P.T. rampaging around adrift in a rough sea whipped by a wind which at times reached moderate gale force: *Mediator* stood by it and made a determined to secure this danger to shipping, eventually succeeding.

Lieut Cdr   **H.M.S. MEDIATOR**   1956/59
pennant no. A.125
Fleet Tug, Mediterranean, attached to
H.M.S. St Angelo and under the operational
Command of C in C Med.

Captain, H.M.S. St Angelo - Captain The Earl of Roden

- - - - - - - - - - -

Commanding Officer	-	Lieut Cdr P.A.C. Day
First Lieutenant	-	Lieut Cdr E. E. Gash
Engineer Officer	-	C.E.R.A. R. Atkinson
Gunner	-	Lieut E. Phillips
relieved by	-	Lieut Bogey Knight
Bos'un	-	Sub Lieut A. Macrae
relieved by	-	Sub Lieut B. Houghton
Sub Lieut	-	Sub Lieut Jim Laurie R.N.V.R.
relieved by	-	Sub Lieut Tony Doyle R.N.V.R.

H.M.S.MEDIATOR (7 Bustler class) (4ᵗʰ ship of the name 1745)

Ocean Rescue Tug.

Laid down 21ˢᵗ June 1944. Built by Henry Robb of Leith.

Displacement 1800 tons. Length 205 ft X 38½ ft X 17 ft. No Armament in peace time but during hostilities 1 X 3 inch A.A.Gun,1 X 2 pdr Pom Pom, 2 X 20 mm A.A., 2 Lewis guns

Machinary 2 sets Polar Diesels driving a single screw. 400 B.H.P. = 15 knots

Oil Fuel 405 tons Diesel

Complement 43 (5 Officers and 38 Ratings of whom 25 were Maltese).

Above: Fig 72 *Mediator* in dry dock in Malta Dockyard, 1957.

Left: Fig 71 The officers involved along with P.A.C. Day while he was in command of HMS *Mediator*, with a basic specification of the ship.

The story began when *Mediator* called in at Bighi Bay to pick up her Battle Practice Target (B.P.T) and proceeded to an exercise area to the west of the Island. In position Mediator got the full treatment from the elements — the B.P.T was heeling over at an angle of 40 degrees in a north-westerly moderate gale. *Mediator* herself was bucking quite rapidly.

The American battleship USS *Iowa* in the exercise area opened fire with her secondary turrets. During the practice and for about forty minutes after the exercise had commenced things began happening onboard the B.P.T. The target's fore-mast snapped and went over the side, taking with it about 65 percent of the lattice-work on the target. This was adjudged to be the effect of the weather with the shooting as a secondary consideration.

USS *Iowa* then began shooting with her big 16-inch guns. Five minutes later it was seen that the B.P.T. had parted her tow and was wallowing out of control in the rough sea.

The towing pendant was considered to have parted through a fluke shot clipping the wire.

Mediator stood by the B.P.T during the day — a risky business as the target sported a bow similar in appearance to an A-Class submarine and probably a lot sharper. At about 4pm that afternoon the ship was manoeuvred close enough for two men – Petty Officer J.H. Lockhart DSM of the Target Marking Party, and Able Seaman T. Foyston – to leap onto the switch-backing B.P.T. They secured a six-inch manilla rope onto the target, but with both the target and *Mediator* rolling and pitching violently it snapped.

Undaunted the two men on the B.P.T., soaked to the skin and washed down by icy spray and green water, got another pendent across from Mediator. This time through the manoeuvring of *Mediator* in attempting to keep the range reduced between the ship and B.P.T., the wire was apparently cut by the Fleet tug's propeller. No damage was immediately apparent to the screw after Lieutenant Commander Day had informed his Engineering Officer, C.E.R.A.R. Atkinson.

After almost two hours on the charging B.P.T. the two men were well-nigh overcome with the cold and wet: they were taken back inboard, and *Mediator* continued to stand by the target until nightfall.

Came the night and more trouble. The darkness was intense and with the demolition of the target's lattice-work, *Mediator* was having difficulty finding the partly submerged target on her radar. By daylight there was no sign of the target. A sea search was carried out and *Mediator's* commander requested that an air search be carried out.

Roving aircraft from HMS *Falcon* reported sighting the target later in the morning.

With three American destroyers close by her position *Mediator* closed the position and found the target drifting beam on to the wind. Lieutenant Commander Day took the Fleet Tug close in by going astern from down wind. This kept the ship away from the pitching knife-edge bows of the B.P.T. and avoided serious damage even though at this stage the wind and sea had diminished considerably.

Shortly after mid-day Able Seaman E. Houghton and Able Seaman P. Parker jumped onto the target followed soon after by Able Seaman C. Bougeard. The trio, in the words of their skipper, "Had little difficulty in hauling across a new wire," and 25 minutes after the men had jumped onto the B.P.T. the tow was connected.

Back in harbour it was found that in going astern to maintain close range on the first wild day, the wire in fact had been sliced through by the propeller, according to the diver's reports. It is assumed that this was also responsible for the shipbuilder's tube on the propeller shaft moving forward a fraction of an inch.

1957   PAGE 12.

Times of Malta

Sat 23rd March 1857 - Threepence

1. These photographs, just released by Naval Headquarters, show in dramatic sequence (see story on page 5) the efforts made to recover a battle practice target which broke loose recently in heavy weather from the Fleet tug "Mediator" off Malta and was a danger to shipping. Above: A.B. E. Houghton and A.B. P. Parker stand diminute figures on the bows of the target just before it was finally taken in tow after a 24 hour struggle.

2. The story begins ... The target is hit and breaks loose from the tug. Petty Officer J. H. Lockhart D.S.M. jumps onto the bows of the target, amid swirling waters, and attempts to secure a line between target and tug ....

4. Overcome with cold and miserably wet, Foyston swims in heavy seas towards the tug and climbs inboard. "Mediator" at night tries to keep the target in sight ...

3. Almost hidden by the waves breaking over the target, A.B. T. Foyston hangs on for dear life. But the 6-inch manilla rope finally secured to the tug snaps and later a wire also parts. Lockhart and Foyston are called back to the tug before nightfall ...

Fig 73 Four cuttings from *The Times of Malta*'s article about *Mediator*'s battle target tow shenanigans.

1957

5. Next day the target is lost but is later located by an aircraft and A.B. E. Houghton, A.B. P. Parker and A.B. C. Bougeard jump onto the target from "Mediator". Finally a wire is connected between the target and the tug which tows it back to Grand Harbour.

Fig 74 The fifth cutting from the article.

Thus ended a very tricky episode for *Mediator*: signals of congratulations on seamanship and personal efforts in this operation which saved a potential danger to shipping from becoming an effective menace on the High Seas were later received from Admiral Sir Ralph Edwards Commander in Chief Mediterranean, Rear Admiral W.G. Brittain, Flag Officer Malta and Vice Admiral C.R. Brown Cdr 6th Fleet.

The following article was first seen in *The Times of Malta* dated 20 August 1957, written by J.P. Scicluna, and it is reproduced here from copy notes in Lieutenant Commander Day's scrap-book of his time on HMS *Mediator*.

When the big guns fire

The glassy calm sea was suddenly rent with explosions as a line of splashes mushroomed on both sides of the battle practice target. On board the target towing tug, cine cameras hummed as they took pictures, recording the fall of shot.

Four miles away on the port quarter of the fleet tug HMS *Mediator*, was the trials cruiser HMS *Cumberland* preparing for another shoot, with the new guns which she is testing before they will be mounted on future ships of the Royal Navy.

That shoot was to be delayed by some 20 minutes, for a keen lookout on the tug's bridge had spotted a fishing boat lying plumb in a position where a ricochet may end its flight. The huge red flag indicating that the area was

 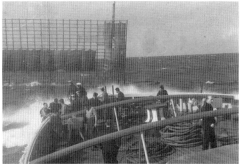

Left: **Fig 75** HMS *Mediator* taking the battle practice target in tow in Grand Harbour, 1957.

Right: **Fig 76** The US battleship *Iowa* inadvertently cut the tow rope of the battle practice target with a shell from her 15-inch guns, and HMS *Mediator* had to recover the target.

Left: **Fig 77** Approaching the battle practice target stern first.

Right: Fig 78 A Maltese AB jumping from the stern of HMS *Mediator* down onto the target in order to reconnect the tow.

clear of shipping was dipped and cruiser, tug and target shaped course to keep the *luzzu* and its crew out of harm's way.

A full job —

That is just one little example of what may happen whenever ships of the Royal Navy fire their guns off Malta.

It is practically an everyday occasion for even as far out as 25 miles, one is bound to meet a fishing boat and it is usually lying in the direct line of fire. It is worse at night in choppy weather when small craft are difficult to discern.

Target towing tugs leave Grand Harbour on an average of four times per week in all weathers. Two Royal Navy tugs, HMS *Mediator* and HMS *Brigand*, tow all sorts of targets night and day.

They have to be at the right place at the right time and steaming at the right speed. HMS *Mediator* which is commanded by Lieutenant Commander P.A.C. Day of Fareham, Hants, is one of the most modern and biggest tugs afloat. Built to merchant navy standards, *Mediator* is also one of the most comfortable ships of the Royal Navy, where accommodation is concerned. There are so many cabins available that even the able seamen use them.

Two-thirds of her ships company is composed of Maltese ratings — in fact all ratings except the technical type are Maltese. They are proud of their ship and speak highly of their Officers.

This compliment was returned by the Officers who said that Maltese sailors are hard working and seldom give them any trouble.

They are the inveterate rivals of the ship's company of HMS *Brigand* which is commanded by Lieutenant Commander W.A. Arrow. Both ships' companies think they are the best.

Backroom Boys —

Brigand is of course an older and smaller ship and is not as well equipped as *Mediator*. While *Brigand* has conventional engines *Mediator* has two diesel engines which propel a single screw and give her a range of thousands of miles. Diesel engines also make up for the cleanliness which is very much evident on *Mediator*.

Both ships have done long towing jobs — they both towed landing craft to Gibraltar. Both tugs are on call for any salvage operation that may come up.

Mediator by the way is with the Fleet on Summer Cruise and is spending some days in Augusta, Palermo and Trapani.

But now let us turn to the other side of the picture. It is not only the tug that makes target firing possible. There are the men of the Fleet Target Marking Party based on HMS *Ricasoli* who are the backroom boys of the organisation.

For all their brave title, the Fleet Target Marking Party consists of one Officer and 14 men. Lieutenant A.E. Millham, a Welshman, is the Fleet Target Officer and he briefly explained to me what their work is, on board *Mediator* as she steamed out to the firing positions the other day.

They are responsible for maintaining the targets in the best possible condition which means continuous work, as invariably targets get smashed almost every time a firing takes place.

Maintenance —

They have to repair all the damage, replacing broken spars and towing points. Whenever the hull of the target is damaged, however, it is a dockyard job to repair it.

They have a variety of targets to take care of, from the big Battle Practice Target which weighs around 400 tons to American High Speed Target Mark IX, the British Mark X, splash targets, the Hong Kong Targets and the smallest of them all—the Larne—which weighs less than a hundred weight. Of the fifteen people that make up the party, seven are United Kingdom personnel.

At sea, personnel from the Fleet Target Marking Party go onboard the towing tug, where their job is to record the fall of shot, especially pre-action calibration shots.

They use an instrument called "The Rake" because it is shaped like a rake. It is a piece of wood with nails spaced evenly with smaller nails in between. The big square between the large nails marks a distance of 50 yards and the space between the small nail and the bigger one is 25 yards.

On return to HMS *Ricasoli* the Fleet Target Marking Party sends a record of the shoot to the Commanding Officer of the ship, the Fleet Gunnery Officer and the Gunnery Officer to the Flag Officer Second in Command. In the case of submarines a record is sent to the Captain 1st Submarine Squadron. When rapid firing is taking place then cine-cameras have to be used.

Wet Work —

It is not only the Royal Navy that shoots at the targets off Malta. The United States Navy joins in while the Royal Air Force and the United States Navy patrol squadron based at Hal Far frequently call for targets.

Right-hand man to Lieutenant Millham is Petty Officer James N. Lockhart of Glasgow who won a DSM in Korea when he was in HMS *Charity*'s director when she shelled a Communist ammunition train and blew it to pieces.

Last February P.O. Lockhart was one of the personnel who managed to re-connect the tow between the remains of a B.P.T. and the ship when the target broke adrift in a gale after a shell had parted the towing wire.

On another occasion, Petty Officer Lockhart and his men recovered another target, which broke adrift and was sailing by itself. They were transferred from *Mediator* to the target in heavy seas.

After considerable difficulty during which time they were repeatedly submerged by heavy seas breaking over the target, the tow was re-connected. It was considered too dangerous to recover the men from the target—it was blowing Force 7—so *Mediator* set course for Grand Harbour, while the Target Party secured themselves between the lattice work and the sail—a strip of black cloth which runs the length of the B.P.T. to assist firing ships officers in sighting the target—and they remained in this position for the three-hour journey home.

Men of the Fleet Marking Party like the men of the tugs are likely to be called out by day and night.

Firing may be taking place just a couple of miles out, it may be 25 miles or more. The job may take a few hours, or it may take a few days, but just the same, they go on doing one of the most unglamorous yet important jobs which have an important bearing on the efficiency of the Navy.

All in a day's work for the ship and her commanding officer, although when the huge 16-inch guns of USS *Iowa* opened up even with the target half a mile astern this could be more than close enough, such was the power when the live ammunition exploded.

The Royal Navy also had many large guns in the arsenal with many large cruisers still in service, most with multi-turrets of 5-inch or 6-inch guns. Not something you wish to be close to when firing begins – but that was one of the main duties of HMS *Mediator* in the Mediterranean when stationed in Malta during this time.

Naval towing work was all part of a day's work for *Mediator*; she was one of the largest and most powerful tugs in the fleet, and could, if paired with another of the other Bustler class, have towed anything floating during the 1950s.

The Royal Navy had a far larger fleet during these times and so also had a high turnover of ships; for various reasons ships were mothballed or slated for the breakers' yards, and once stripped of the useful equipment and armament would need to be towed to their destination.

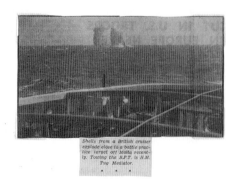 

Left: Fig 79 Another cutting from *The Times of Malta*.

Right: **Fig 80** HMS *Mediator* visiting Marseilles (now Marseille).

Upper left: Fig 81 *Manxman* about to be taken in tow by *Mediator* from Grand Harbour, Valletta, to Gibraltar.

Upper right: Fig 82 *Mediator* towing Manxman from Malta to Gibraltar.

Left:Fig 83 *Mediator* with *Manxman* astern, alongside in Gibraltar harbour.

The following pictures from Lieutenant Commander Day show *Mediator* on general towing duties from one end of the Mediterranean to the other.

As naval towing duties continued at a time when the Royal Navy still had a great many vessels to try and keep maintained, finance dictated that many ships would not be kept on; some were mothballed in reserve while others would be towed to the scrapyards who would have purchased them at bargain prices.

So, the naval tugs were kept busy for a while, and HMS *Mediator* was engaged in many tows including the movement of many Landing Ship Tanks (LSTs) back and forth through the Suez Canal.

Mediator was also a rescue tug, as can be seen from this story carried in *The Times of Malta* 30 January 1959, by a staff reporter, as follows:

Adele Andalo's Last Voyage

Six Survivors safe in Malta after 38 hours adrift

The six survivors from the 845-ton Italian vessel "Adel Andalo" which sunk in a storm some 40 miles south of Malta on Tuesday night arrived in Malta in the Royal Navy tug *Mediator* on Thursday night.

Fig 84 Lowering the whaler to make sure everything is all right on the tow.

Fig 85 LST (Landing Ship, Tank) *Buttress* under tow.

Fig 86 From *Mediator*, passing through the Suez Canal towards Aden.

Fig 87 *Mediator* transiting the Gulf of Suez southbound to Aden.

Above: Fig 88 Towing Lifting Craft 27 from Aden to Malta.

Right: **Fig 89** *Mediator* transiting the Suez Canal northwards with LC 27 secured alongside.

The body of one member of the crew who was reported to have died just 10 minutes before the men in the boat were rescued was also brought ashore from the tug and taken in a naval ambulance to King George V Hospital.

The survivors are suffering from shock but with no visible injuries.

For 38 hours they had fought for their lives against all the might and fury of the sea, bobbing about in a 14-foot dory-type boat.

They bailed water as fast as it was coming in, it seemed like eternity.

One man, on being rescued, was convinced they had been in the boat for three days.

Despite the sheer tragedy of the disaster, the survivors were picked up after a series of lucky chances. Their S.O.S. on Tuesday was made on a hand-operated radio set but several stations, including Cable & Wireless at Malta, Port Lyautey in Morocco, Taranto Radio and Naples Radio picked up the message.

Hopes Fading

The Tug *Mediator* was ordered to sail from Grand Harbour immediately and later on Wednesday morning the minesweepers *Kildarton* and *Dufton* sailed to the search area. R.A.F. and USAAF joined in the search as well as the aircraft carrier *Centaur*.

The search proved futile at first and *Mediator* which was co-ordinating the search, signalled Naval Headquarters — "Search since dawn for *Adel Andalo* by *Mediator* and Shackleton aircraft has produced no sign of ship wreckage nor survivors. Weather, sea moderate, Wind north force four. Do not consider anything can be gained by continuous search after dark."

Boat Sighted

Mediator was carrying out the last leg of her search when the First Lieutenant, Lieut Comdr, E.E. Gash of Boston, Lincs, thought he sighted a boat some one mile away. *Mediator* proceed towards it and came upon seven people in a small 14-foot boat, bailing out water for all they were worth. A.B. Anthony Spiteri of Carmel Street, Zabbar, jumped into the boat despite personal danger and helped the exhausted survivors to be hauled aboard—as soon as this was done the small boat sank.

The survivors said that their dead comrade had died only ten minutes before. Personnel on *Mediator* applied artificial respiration but to no avail.

The boat had drifted some 40 miles from the scene of the sinking when found by *Mediator*.

The captain of the tug, Lieutenant Commander P.A.C. Day, said: "We searched a lot of ocean and saw a boat about 12:30 yesterday. We had been on the search for 33 hours and the crew, five Officers and 32 men of whom two-thirds are Maltese, were constantly on the go."

Ambulances were waiting at the wharf when *Mediator* came in and berthed beside the tug *Brigand*.

Father A. Borg, the Naval Chaplain, was at the wharf together with Sig. Nunzio Lobrano and Sig. Domenico Catalogna of the Italian Consulate to meet the survivors in bitterly cold weather. The six men, well wrapped in blankets, walked or were carried ashore into ambulances.

Air Operation

The Captain of *Adel Andalo,* one of the survivors, was reported to be on his last trip before retiring from the sea.

The aerial side of this rescue operation consisted of aircraft of the Royal Air Force, Fleet Air Arm and United States Navy, operating from Malta and Tripoli: the total flying hours put in during search and rescue operations amounted to almost 90 hours.

The rescue co-ordination centre at Royal Air Force station Luca took over control at 5 a.m. Wednesday morning, and scrambled a search and rescue Shackleton Long-Range maritime recognisance aircraft to the area where it carried out a general search.

This was soon backed up by a second Shackleton, thereby expanding the search area. Three Naval Fireflies from HMS *Falcon* came under R.A.F. control in the search area later in the day. One Shackleton continued the first day's search far into Wednesday night.

Wreckage Sighted

On Thursday the Americans from Wheelus Field sent out a C.54 and a Grumman Albatross amphibious aircraft to comb the general area: the Royal Air Force, again controlling the search from the Malta Rescue co-ordination centre, sortied two Shackletons while the Americans from Hal Far sent out a Neptune patrol bomber.

It was an American Neptune which signalled that it had sighted wreckage and gave the first definite indications that the *Adel Andalo* had indeed sunk.

This wreckage was sighted at 10:30 a.m. and concentrated the search area considerably. A sunken lifeboat was found but no people in it.

Flying conditions in the area were at times extremely bad, with thunder-

Survivors Land from Naval Tug

Angelo Magliolo, the captain of the Italian vessel "Adele Andalo," is carried ashore at Parlatorio Wharf in H.M. Dockyard from the tug "Mediator," which rescued him and five other survivors after the ship sank south of Malta on Tuesday night. Father A. Borg (left), and officials of the Italian Consulate, met the survivors. (Story on page 3).

TIMES OF MALTA
SATURDAY, January 31, 1959   Threepence

A survivor from the "Adele Andalo" is helped towards a Naval ambulance. With five other survivors he spent 38 hours in a small open boat, at the mercy of heavy seas.

Fig 90 Clippings from *The Times of Malta*, 31 January 1959.

storms and poor visibility adding to the searchers' troubles. Despite this the air search continued after *Mediator* had turned back to Malta with the survivors on board, as the R.C.C. were not yet satisfied that there were definitely no more survivors.

C in C's Thanks

The search, in which Skyraiders and Helicopters from the aircraft carrier *Centaur* took an active part, was eventually abandoned at dusk on Thursday night. All the time more Helicopters from H.M.S. *Falcon* were standing by at immediate readiness should they have been required.

Thanks came in from the Commander in Chief Mediterranean to all British vessels involved.

Lieutenant Commander Day's story continues:

As we rolled into May 1959 it was time for me to relinquish my command of the rescue tug HMS *Mediator*. I had obtained approval from the Commander in Chief Mediterranean that Betty my wife should be allowed to travel overnight in HMS *Mediator*. She slept in the sick bay!!!

The ship was to escort the Royal Navy Yacht Race from Malta to Syracuse in Sicily, my relief would be onboard, and I would hand over my command of HMS *Mediator* to him on the jetty at Syracuse.

So, all was arranged for Betty and I to travel overland back to the United Kingdom. Our heavy baggage had already been dispatched to the UK and our car, an Austin A50, was duly hoisted onboard the ship using our own derrick and it would be landed by the same method on arrival at Syracuse. This all went according to plan.

I had a happy and successful two and a half years in command of HMS *Mediator* based on Malta, although we varied our presence between Aden and Gibraltar. We had on board a fine crew which consisted of four Officers (apart from myself) and 38 ratings of whom the more junior members were 25 Maltese.

In 1964 *Mediator* arrived back at Plymouth, where the Admiralty, deeming her surplus to requirements, offered her up for sale. Greek shipping was growing at a furious rate, to become one of the powerhouses of world shipping, and *Mediator*, having been based in the Mediterranean all those years, was well known to Greek ship-owners. So in February 1965 she was sold to Greek shipping interests in the form of Tsavliris (Salvage and Towage) Ltd of Piraeus, and renamed *Nisos Zakynthos*. Then in 1975 she was sold on to Maritime Commercial Enterprises Ltd and renamed *Atlas*. In 1985 she was struck from Lloyd's register.

The following are some comments that were sent into my old website and blog on Leith-built ships, from ex-crew and interested people, reproduced here unabridged.

Left: Fig 91 The Days' car loaded onto *Mediator* in Malta Dockyard, 22 May 1959 (photo reproduced by kind permission of Captain K.J.C. Day).

Right: Fig 92 In 1975 *Mediator*, renamed *Atlas* (photo, RFA Plymouth).

Fig 93 HMRT *Mediator* leaving the Henry Robb Shipyard at Leith just after her build in late 1944 (image from my collection).

Joseph Chircop

My father, Alfred Chircop, known as Alf, served on this ship till his retirement and subsequently migrating to Australia in 1963. This ship was involved in the Suez Canal conflict. My father had served 6 years in the army and 21 years in the Navy in Malta. But he never mentioned anything that happened on board. The one and only time was when they were fired upon by the Egyptians.

Tom Mayfield

In 1963 I was a newly qualified RN Electrical Artificer based with the minesweeping squadron at Msida Base and then HMS *St. Angelo*, Malta. *Mediator* shared the support ship duties with RFA Sea Salvor, when the minesweepers were on their regular sweepex's around the Med. One particularly memorable night in the midst of a full gale off the Italian coast, we were woken when the engines stopped and we lost all power. *Mediator*, like her sisters, was prone to heavy rolling in even a slight sea, and it was a somewhat nail biting few hours before the engines came back on and power was resumed. I did at least two trips in her and it was always a pleasure to join her crew.

We had some interesting trios around the Med during my 2 years in Malta. Long time ago, but I seem to remember them saying it was the large amount of diesel fuel they carried that made the rolling worse as it was used up. Also, again memory, I think that the fuel tanks weren't broken up by baffles to prevent "sloshing". Sorry no photos, just some happy memories

Yours aye,

Tom

David Lane

Mediator was used for launching PTA as targets for HMS *Aisne* in SeaCat trials in October 1962, Lieutenant Bob Fenton was in charge of the PTA team, based I believe at Hal Far.

Clive Reynolds

I served on *Mediator* during my national service as stoker/mechanic 1st class 1949–1950. I have loads of tales to tell and would love to hear from anyone who is interested in knowing more or anyone who was there when I was. I remember a colleague called Munton who came from Rutland.

Richard A Judd

I served as the REM on her from November 1962 until she went back to Plymouth. She had a ships dog, Cholmondely, we had to raise money for him to be quarantined in the UK, the crew were Maltese stokers and seamen.

Colin Davies

My late Father, John Davies, served on her I believe when she was HMS. He would often say they were some of his fondest 12 yrs of RN service

Alan Lewis

(From 2017) my father Alan Lewis served as a navigator's yeoman and Qm on board from 1949 to 1951. Now aged 86 still fondly remembers Lt Cdr C Stamford and served in the Middle and Far East.

8: *REWARD*

During 1943 Henry Robb's shipyards were building as fast as they could, with a dozen warships such as corvettes and frigates going down the ways. They also launched three much-needed cargo ships during this year.

As soon as one ship was launched the keel blocks would be set out for the next build. In 1944, a couple of months after the keel had been laid for *Mediator*, her sister ship was laid down, on 6th April.

As her keel took shape her after collision bulkhead would be horned up into place on the slipway, then her frames going forward until she was ready to be plated.

Almost eight months to the day she was ready for launch, as Ship No 336 in the shipyard order book.

With the breaking of a bottle of champagne over her bow by Mrs Holden, she was named HMS *Reward*. After she went into the water on 13 October to be towed around to the fitting-out basin, her fitting out took the same five months as that of her sister.

She was not completed, however, and in service with the Royal Navy until March 1945; as the war entered its final phases the need to concentrate on the larger frigates was deemed priority.

Fig 94 HMS *Reward*, armed and ready (image copyright unknown).

Fig 95 RFA *Reward* at Malta (image from Historical RFA).

She would sail into action under the pennant number W 164. One of her first tasks was as part of the liberation fleet that would take the Channel Islands back from German control. So on 4 May 1945 she became part of Force 135 for Operation Nestegg, along with HMRT *Growler*.

Then by the 22nd of the month *Reward* had sailed from Liverpool in Convoy OS 130KM until it dispersed on the 24th. *Growler* was with the same convoy. *Reward* was heading for the Far East fleet, but fortunately, with the dropping of the second atomic bomb on Japan on 9 August 1945 that country surrendered and the world war was over for most.

Back in home waters *Reward* was involved in the rescue of the steamer *Josiah P. Cressey* which had a flooded engine room; she was towed safely into Fishguard harbour.

Into 1947 *Reward* would find the waters around her a bit warmer as she sailed from Bombay on 20 March alongside HMS *Mediator*. They were towing the Admiralty Floating Dock (ADF 35) to Malta. With the codename Operation Snow White, the two tugs and their large charge arrived at Aden on 3 April. Proceeding through the Suez Canal they arrived at Port Said on the 14th, then on through the Mediterranean, arriving at Malta on 8 May. Valletta, and most of the small island of Malta, were trying to rebuild after being on the end of some of the most sustained bombing of World War II; the harbour was still being cleared of sunken ships, along with the sunken ADF 8.

HMS *Reward* was back in home water when she towed the huge battleship HMS *Nelson* from Portsmouth up to Rosyth in October 1947; *Nelson* was being placed on the reserve list.

Through the 1950s HMS *Reward* spent most of her time going back and forth to and from the Mediterranean. She took part in the Home Fleet's spring cruise around the Mediterranean in 1951, before returning to be laid up at the Royal Dockyard during 1952. She was then transferred to Pembroke Dock, before taking part in the Queen Elizabeth II's Coronation Fleet Review at Spithead in June 1953.

She would then sail for Invergordon to take part in the Home Fleet's autumn cruise; she took part in Operation Mariner as part of this cruise.

During early 1954 she was back in the Mediterranean, this time to Tangier with HMS *Superb* and other units of the Royal Navy, taking part in the Home Fleet's spring training.

Fig 96 RFA *Reward*.
Photo from RFAA
Plymouth.

In spring 1960 HMS *Reward* was transferred back to Malta for service with the Target Squadron based there. This time she was the one who arrived at the island in tow, pulled by tug *Agile*.

By 1 May 1962 HMS *Reward* had been chartered by the United Towing Company Ltd, Hull, who promptly renamed her *Englishman*. One year later she was taken over by the Royal Fleet Auxiliary and renamed RFA *Reward*, with pennant number A 264.

During December 1964 RFA *Reward*, under Captain A.W. Jewers, who had been appointed as master in November 1963, was in collision with an East German ship, *Stralsund*. In June 1968 Captain D. Hazell was appointed as *Reward*'s master.

The next notable event in the story of RFA *Reward* was not to happen until 1970 when she was transferred to the Port Auxiliary Service (PAS) as *Reward*. In May 1970 she was used to tow HMS *Troubridge* to the breaker's yard at Newport, before being placed in reserve in October 1972.

Reward was now laid up going nowhere while the Admiralty pondered what to do with the ship. She was not alone, however, as, what with the Cold War settling down into the stalemate that formed the Eastern Bloc and the West she was now, along with many others, seen as either obsolete or just not required any more.

In January 1975 *Reward* arrived at the Royal Dockyard at Chatham for conversion, a decision having been made to turn her into a naval patrol ship. Six months later she sailed

Fig 97 HMS *Reward* when part of the Fishery Protection Squadron (© Aage Schjølberg acknowledged).

from Chatham for the Port Edgar naval base at South Queensferry in the Firth of Forth, just along from her place of build at Leith. Her conversion into naval patrol ship now complete, she was commissioned at Port Edgar as HMS *Reward*, with Lieutenant Commander Angus Sandford RN in command.

HMS *Reward* would be used in the fishery protection role and to help make sure that the ever-growing oil rigs in the North Sea were also protected. The 1970s was a time of what was to become known as the Irish Troubles, with the constant threat to life and limb from the IRA in Northern Ireland and the south. The oil rigs were a target for many threats, and each one had to be monitored. So on 25 August HMS *Reward* provided a headquarters and support for the Scotland and Northern Ireland Explosive Ordnance Team. This team's extremely dangerous job was to go and check out the threats when received. They checked, for example, the Phillips Petroleum gas rigs off Great Yarmouth when information received had told of charges planted by the terrorist group.

Then on 10 August 1976 *Reward* was involved in a collision in the Firth of Forth with the German container ship SS *Plainsman*. In very thick fog the *Plainsman* hit *Reward* just aft of midships, almost breaking her in half. Fortunately there were no fatalities nor even injuries, but *Reward* sank pretty quickly. I well remember the fog around the firth; when I worked at the Leith shipyards visibility could sometimes be down to no more than 10 feet. Out in the firth the fog would be even thicker.

Now a salvage operation was required, and the Navy had to bring in the civilian floating crane *Brunel* to lift the shattered tug from below the water; with just her bridge and funnel

Fig 98 Floating crane *Brunel* in position, getting ready to raise HMS *Reward* from her watery end. Note the mooring/salvage vessel in the background, which may well have been RMAS *Goosander*, another ship built at the Henry Robb Shipyard, and stationed at Rosyth after a time in the Falklands during that campaign. (Image from Historical RFA.)

Fig 99 HMS *Reward* (previously RFA *Reward*) being raised (image from Historical RFA).

still showing clear of the water, she presented a danger to shipping. By 29 August she had been raised and beached close by, and it did not take long to see that the ship was a constructive loss; and she was sold to Jas White & Co. Ltd, who loaded the old tug onto a barge to take her to St David's harbour in Wales for demolition.

So ended the career of HMS *Reward*, the sixth in line of the Bustler class ships built at Leith. This was a sad end for another fine Leith-built ship. However, at least HMS *Reward* also had a postage stamp produced featuring her, which is not something most vessels can boast of.

The following are some comments that were sent into my old website and blog on Leith-built ships, from ex-crew and interested people, reproduced here unabridged.

Fig 100 On this postage stamp HMRT *Reward* is shown off the Seychelles in World War II, with HMS *Belfast* and HMS *Rapid*. (Image from my collection.)

Bill Cowie

Served on *Reward* based in Malta from 1960/62. All the senior rates & leading hands were British, all the seamen & engine room junior ratings were Maltese. We brought her back to Chatham in Feb 62 & paid off; the same month she was transferred to the RFA (I think), the last time I saw her was in Aden in 1965.

Dennis Walker

My service number is C/SKX 892178. Served as ME1 on *Reward* during 1954 and 1956. Would be pleased to hear from anyone who also served on her during this time.

Steve Gibson

Served on board 1975–76 my final draft before leaving RN. i was navigator's yeoman, had some great times carrying out fishery protection. Skipper was Angus Samford LTCom.

Tony Gutteridge

I worked on the *Reward* when she was in dry dock at Chatham Dockyard in 1963, as an electrical fitter apprentice. I think she was in the same dry dock that at present houses HMS *Cavalier* in Chatham Historic Dockyard. May even have been the place where HMS *Victory* was built.

9: *TURMOIL*

The seventh in line of the mighty tugs built at Leith would perhaps end up the most famous of the eight Bustler class ships.

Her keel was laid down in July 1944, just after the invasion of France; her build at ten months took a little bit longer than that of her predecessors.

She was launched from the yard on 11 May 1945 as Ship No 337, named *Turmoil* by Mrs George T.C.P. Swabey.

When she was towed around to the fitting-out basin the war in Europe was over, the Germans having unconditionally surrendered on the 8th of that month. So it was to great relief of the attending crowd that she at least would not be going into action as her six sisters had – but she could still end up in the Far East, as the war with Japan was still going on.

After fitting out and completion of her sea trials she was commissioned into the Royal Navy as HMRT *Turmoil,* and she was to be stationed at Leith for now. She would have the pennant number W 169.

Left: Fig 101 *Turmoil* (photo sent to me by Historical RFA and shown by permission).

Right: Fig 102 *Turmoil* seen here tied up at Malta (photo credit unknown: shown here with kind permission of RFAA Plymouth).

One of her first jobs was to tow SS *Princessa* from the Bristol Channel to Avonmouth under the escort of HMS *Burghead Bay*.

HMRT *Turmoil* was to remain at Leith for only a further year before she was chartered out to Chartered Overseas Towage & Salvage Co. Ltd of London, where she would retain the name *Turmoil*.

On 6 November she sailed from Falmouth, called out to aid her sister *Bustler* along with aircraft from Gibraltar in the search for the lost Brazilian battleship *São Paulo* with her skeleton crew of eight men. On 27 November the search was, however, called off and the ship presumed lost. (For more on this story see Chapter 4.)

THE STORY OF *FLYING ENTERPRISE*

At the start of 1952 *Turmoil* was involved in the attempt to rescue the tramp steamer *Flying Enterprise*, an event that at the time was daily news to the people of Britain, with pressmen on every available ship trying to cover the story.

What had begun as just another relatively standard voyage in December 1951 from Hamburg to America in the old World War II Liberty ship *Flying Enterprise* would soon

Left: Fig 103 *Turmoil* stands off the sinking *Flying Enterprise*. (Photo from the old Leith Shipyard book.)

Right: Fig 104 *Turmoil* once more gets in close to *Flying Enterprise*; she manages to get a line onto the crippled ship. (Image from my collection.)

Fig 105 Left: a US destroyer closes in to pass hot coffee; right: *Flying Enterprise* takes a sheer out to starboard. (Image from *Leith-built Ships on War Service*.)

Fig 106 *Flying Enterprise* (image, Leigh Bishop).

capture the attention of the world. This was in a time when very few people had a television, and the vast majority of people got their news from radio and newspapers, or once a week from the Pathé News at the local cinema.

Flying Enterprise had left Hamburg with, according to her manifest, a cargo of 1,300 tons of pig iron and 900 tons of coffee. She also had ten passengers on board. She was owned by Isbrandtsen Shipping Co. of New York, and she was the second vessel to take this name. Her captain was Henrik Kurt Carlsen.

As the ship left Germany and voyaged through the English Channel, she was soon to be thrown into high drama that would cause a media frenzy that no journalist worth his salt could ignore.

On the night of 25 December she was hit by a storm with seas running at around 40 feet; the storm raged on through the next day, with winds increasing in force. During the next night, Captain Carlsen decided to heave to as the winds continued to increase and were indeed approaching Hurricane Force 12.

Then a crack in the ship's fabric started opening almost amidships. Cracks were not that unusual in the hastily built Liberty ships – but this crack then ran across the main deck and down each side of the hull for around 12 feet. The engine room started flooding. The ship was caught in the storm some 400 miles from Land's End, well into the Atlantic.

During the night of the 27th into the morning of the 28th, with another storm passing by just to the north of the ship, she was rolling up to 20 degrees. Around 11.30 on the morning of the 28th she was hit broadside by a huge wave rolling her 50–70 degrees to port and shifting her cargo, causing her to return to a permanent list of around 30 degrees. Eventually due to the list the engine lost lubrication oil, resulting in the loss of both boilers.

Another crack was soon discovered on the weather deck, and with the ship unable to right herself the captain ordered the radio operator to send out an SOS, which was answered by several ships in the vicinity.

The passengers and crew were rescued by the USS *General A.W. Greely* along with SS *Southland*. The seas were too heavy for their lifeboats to close in on the stricken *Flying Enterprise*, so her passengers and crew had to jump into the raging seas to be picked up by the boats. They all had to swim in the freezing Atlantic, but amazingly just one of the passengers was lost – some reports say this was a Polish crew member – and the lifeboats managed to save all the others.

All, that is, apart from Captain Carlsen, who chose to stay with his ship and await the arrival of a tug. He was to have a long wait, and the world was captivated by the news stories of the brave captain and the attempts to save the ship.

It was the salvage tug *Turmoil* that arrived at the scene on 3 January 1952; *Flying Enterprise* had now been listing badly for five days. It quickly became apparent that it would be impossible for Captain Carlsen, alone aboard the ship, now listing at 60 degrees, to secure a towline on his own.

After several unsuccessful attempts had been made to secure the line, Kenneth Dancy, the 27-year-old chief mate on *Turmoil*, leapt from her deck onto the railing of *Flying Enterprise* on one of the very close approaches made by Captain Dan Parker, master of *Turmoil*, in one of the failed attempts to secure the line. With the help of the chief mate, K. Darcy, a line was secured on the ship and the long difficult tow towards Falmouth could now begin.

By now, due to the ship's easterly drift, it was estimated that she was some 300 miles from Falmouth. This would still, however, be a long and difficult tow with the ship listing so badly in the long Atlantic swell; with the ship shearing first to one quarter then the other, they were making headway at only around 3 knots.

Then on 8 January another storm hit the ships, forcing *Turmoil* to heave to just 60 miles from safety. But *Flying Enterprise* was now listing at 80 degrees, lying ever deeper in the water.

Then the next day the towline parted, and with the ship now showing signs of breaking up Captain Carlsen and Dancy were forced to jump from her funnel into the sea. They were picked up by *Turmoil* as the crew watched the doomed vessel sink slowly under the water, her bow seeming to take a last look around before disappearing into the icy ocean depths.

Despite the 'no cure, no pay' contract, the Isbrandtsen Line very generously awarded the crew of *Turmoil* £2,500 to share amongst themselves. On 5 June that year Captain Parker was awarded the MBE.

Two years later *Turmoil* was involved in another huge tow featuring a feat of skilful seamanship when on 30 November 1954 she towed the stern portion of the Liberian tanker *World Concord* to the Clyde after she had broken in two. (Originally, she was to have towed the tanker to Liverpool, but that port refused her entry.) The tanker was eventually put back together again and continued to sail the seven seas.

Sadly, it was reported in the *New York Times* of 9 August 1955 that Captain Frederick D. Parker MBE was discharged dead, having fallen from the bridge of *Turmoil*.

In 1957 *Turmoil* was transferred to the RFA and, being the second ship of that name used by the RFA, was renamed RFA *Turmoil (2)*.

In 1961 she was given a major refit at Ardrossan Dockyard, but was then laid up at Pembroke Dock before being sold in 1965 to a Greek company, Tsavliris Salvage and Towage at Piraeus, and renamed *Nisos Kerkyra*.

She was then sold on once more, staying in Greece, to be purchased by Loucas Matsas & Sons, Piraeus; she was renamed *Matsas* in 1971.

Then in 1986 she was sold for scrap, broken up at Agia Shipyards, Perama.

Fig 107 *Turmoil* as the Greek tug *Matsas* (photo credit unknown).

Although her breaking for scrap was the end of the ship herself, so many memories of her remain; here are just some of the stories from the men who sailed or served on her over the years.

The first tale is from Bert Brown:

> I was on *Turmoil* from the 11/4/57 to 6/9/57. I joined it at Cobh Ireland. That was her station, we had two or three call outs, which was cancelled. After being at sea for two or three days, I always felt safe in rough weather on the *Turmoil*. Then we went down to Trinidad to pick up a 10.000-ton tanker to tow to Rotterdam, it took us approx. 14 days to get there, and 6 weeks to Rotterdam. Approx a week out of Trinidad, one of our lifeboats caught on fire, which we had to drop into the sea, it caught alight from sparks from the funnel. Two nights later we had a fire in the engine room, which we had to fight with wet blankets as most of the fire extinguishers did not work, we got it out ok, But we was down to four knots for a week or more, Time we got to Rotterdam, We was low on food and water. From Rotterdam we sailed for Greenock in Scotland. We were due to go into drydock. On the way we came across a coaster which had broken down, Captain Leckie spoke to them, I don't know the outcome of the talks, but we left them, and went on to Greenock.
>
> I paid off there and signed on the M.V. *Tremorvah*, a cargo ship.
>
> Regards, Bert Brown.
>
> *Turmoil*, A sailor's life for me, would not have missed it for the world.

Bert also sent me some photographs of his time on *Turmoil*.

Left: Fig 108 *Turmoil* tied up at the dockside in Ireland (image, Bert Brown).

Right: Fig 109 Bert Brown (on the right) with some of the crew messing around on *Turmoil* (image, Bert Brown).

Left: Fig 110 Bert Brown on *Turmoil* with a tanker being towed (image, Bert Brown).

Right: Fig 111 *Turmoil* at the dockside, seen from above (image, Bert Brown).

Fig 112 Bert Brown with some fancy headgear on at the ship's wheel on *Turmoil* (image, Bert Brown).

The following is the story of Sean Cowman's short but very eventful time on *Turmoil*.

Six Months on M.T. "Turmoil"

I joined the R.T. "Turmoil" as Second Radio Officer in Falmouth early afternoon on 23.3.1962 after an overnight ferry crossing from Ireland and a long train journey from London. So began six of the most unusual months almost to the day of my sea going career. My first sight of the tug as she sat beside the wharf left me not all that impressed. Her towing deck was level with the quay, and she looked small and a bit ugly.

However, on closer inspection her raked fore and main mast masts made her look fast, her oversized buff funnel made her look powerful and her slightly flared bow and the short distance from her stem to the point where her hull reached full beam width made her look belligerent. Later that afternoon when the tide had dropped, looking down at her from the quay side she just looked ugly and untidy again.

On boarding her, the bosun showed me to the Captain's cabin and over the next few days I tried to get used to life on a ship which was so much different to anything I had sailed on over the previous five years spent on much larger and more opulent vessels of the Indo China Steam Navigation Company out of Hong Kong. The first thing I did was pack away my uniforms since it was obvious they would not be 'wanted on voyage' on a vessel where dress was not only informal but almost optional. It took a while to get used to a captain who wore a trilby hat on the bridge and a Chief Engineer who seemed to live in a boiler suit which had once – probably a century previously – been white but which was now a mass of oil and grease stains.

"Turmoil" was undergoing a minor refit at the time but officially she was on salvage station and a few days later the call came in to say that a Norwegian vessel with the unlikely English name of "Fernhurst" had lost steering somewhere off the notorious "Minkies" (Minquiers) near Jersey.

Many of the crew were ashore and for the next five minutes "Turmoil's" siren boomed around Falmouth harbour calling them back on board: most of them made it and we quickly found ourselves in a full speed race for the casualty against one of United Towing's vessels which, I think, was the "Merchantman". The "Merchantman" was a sister of "Turmoil" (NV) and when we arrived on scene, we found a beautiful modern French tug also standing by so it was two battered British versus a French belle for the job.

We all laid off the casualty for two days hopefully waiting on a Lloyd's open form which never came as the casualty's company signed a contract salvage job with a Belgian towing company leaving us all three with nothing to do but head back to port. This was something I was delighted about as I was totally unused to being almost hove to on an exceedingly small vessel in a lively enough sea. I had spent a lot of time bent over a bucket in the radio room.

When we tied up in Falmouth the ship's agent arrived with a telegram for me saying my then girlfriend – now my wife of over fifty years – had been rushed to hospital in London with an appendix. So I headed for London by train, fortunately having first changed into my uniform, fortunately because on arrival at the hospital at ten o clock the following morning, one look at the uniform and any rules about visiting hours went out the window. My girlfriend having been operated on successfully, I was able to catch a late-night train back to Falmouth where I managed to jump on board just as the "Turmoil" was casting off and heading for Newcastle to pick up some barges for Milford Haven. We picked up the barges all right but never got them to Milford Haven.

Early morning, somewhere southwest of the Isle of Wight a coded message came through for the Captain which resulted in our making a dash for Falmouth where we dropped the barges to a harbour tug and again found ourselves going flat out for Appledore to 'rescue' one of our own vessels, the "Britonia". "Britonia" was under construction in Appledore shipyards which, it was thought, were about to go bankrupt.

The vessel had been launched and was about to finish 'fitting out' but, as ownership of the vessel would be a matter of legal dispute should the shipyard go 'bust' we were tasked with the job of going in and getting her out. This we did in quite a spectacular 'cutting out' operation.

It was a beautiful sunny evening with flat calm seas when we arrived off Appledore, which was fortunate as we had only an hour or so to get across the sand bar at the entrance to the harbour and get back out again. We had to traverse the entire harbour front to reach the shipyard where "Britonia" was tied up. This we did at some considerable speed, sending fishermen and sunbathers scrambling up the rocks for the promenade and leaving moored yachts and pleasure craft heaving in the considerable wake thrown up by our passage. "Turmoil's" engines made quite a lot of noise at speed but so did the sound of our wake crashing on shore.

Nevertheless, the sound of our passage failed to cover the choice language of those scrambling for their lives or being thrown about on their moored harbour craft. To make a long story short, we got alongside the "Britonia", our bosun and a few deckhands hands sent a watchman on his way – not difficult since the bosun was waving a fire axe which might be needed to chop through mooring lines – got a towing wire on board, and in a matter of minutes we were under our way again, much to the chagrin of Appledorians just recovering from our previous transit. One of our crew swore afterwards that he heard someone ashore scream, "J---s C----t, here she comes again and this time there are two of 'em." I do know we heard the sound of a couple of police car sirens and saw the flashing lights as they raced along the promenade.

Anyway, we just about made it across the bar but it must have been a close run thing as we left a pretty large muddy stain on the sea's surface astern as we headed for Milford Haven. The weather was good enough which was fortunate as we had not had time to attach a bridle – two thick nylon lines made fast to the bows of the tow terminating in a steel ring to which the towing wire was attached and which acted as a 'shock absorber' in a sea – to the tow, and being light she was lively. Also, she had no lights, so we had to keep her on a 'short' tow and light her up with our search light if any other vessels came close. On arrival at Milford Haven just before light next morning, under instructions from the ship's agent, we tied "Britonia" up to a mooring buoy, the agent put a crew on board her – possession being nine points of the law – and, having delivered some mail, sent us on our way out to sea before the authorities could get hold of us.

So, we headed south towards "Lands' End for orders" picking up a BBC news broadcast which mentioned something about piracy. A few hours later we received a radio message ordering us to Copenhagen to pick up a T2 tanker mid-section for Baltimore in Maryland USA, and we never did hear anything else about the "Britonia" incident except that we received a message from the "Owners" thanking and congratulating us for our good work.

About 500 T2 tankers were built by the United States during WW2. They were designed primarily to carry oil from the Caribbean and Gulf of Mexico to the US and they performed excellently in this role. However, after the war ended, T2s began to voyage more widely and they soon earned – like their sisters the Liberty ships – a reputation for breaking in two.

Initially it was thought that this was due to faulty ship design or faulty welding because of shipyard welders being paid bonuses for fast work. However, it turned out that the problem was the inferior quality of the steel that had been used in their construction which became excessively brittle in cold weather or low temperature seas. The oil tanks were also subject to corrosion because of the high sulphur content of the Gulf oil that had been carried. The combination of these issues meant that after the war ended the US was left with a lot of ships whose forecastles, centre castle accommodation and bridge structures and engine rooms were perfect, but the hulls were rotten and dangerous.

In the mid-1950s it was decided that as part of the Marshall Plan for the economic reconstruction of Europe, shipyards in Copenhagen, Brest, Cadiz and Genoa would be commissioned to build mid-sections consisting of the entire tank sections of the ships and that these mid-sections would be towed across the Atlantic to the Baltimore and Maryland Dockyards where the old and the new hulls would be laid alongside one another, the old engine rooms, centre and forecastles would be cut from the old hulls, slid across and welded to the new mid-sections and welded into place thus giving a perfectly functioning new T2. It was one of these mid-sections that "Turmoil" was now to collect from Copenhagen.

The mid-section was over 400 feet long, 68 feet beam and weighed under 9,000 gross: it certainly made "Turmoil" tiny by comparison. For the voyage, a steel box was welded amidships on the deck of the mid-section as accommodation for a running crew of six Dutchmen whose job it would be to help should the towline part at any time during the voyage: given that the mid-section was no more than a slab-sided, square ended box, towering about forty feet above the sea, without a running crew it would not have been possible to board to reconnect in the event of a parted towline.

Part of the job of the Radio Officers (Sparks) was to rig a medium wave transceiver with battery power supply and also make sure that the handheld VHF sets were functioning properly so that radio communications between the running crew and the "Turmoil" could be ensured. This was no easy job as no one had thought to provide a mast of some kind to rig an aerial – not to mention navigation lights – and the dockyard seemed reluctant to do anything about this since they claimed that it had not been included in the original contract.

It may also have been that our reputation in Copenhagen was not exactly one of glowing rectitude since our crew were never abstemious in their drinking habits and one of the Dutchmen had stolen a bicycle to make it faster and easier to get around the deck of the mid-section. Also, the prospect of a forty-day trip across the Atlantic on a "dry" ship with 'up spirits' consisting of either a six pack of beer or a noggin of whiskey, together with a bar of chocolate on a Saturday night the only exception, meant that pre-voyage stocking up ashore was required. (Up spirits had to be paid for at the end of the voyage of course.)

Eventually, with much fussing from the harbour tugs, we left Copenhagen, reached the open sea and got under way making about four knots in calm seas. The crossing of the North Sea was uneventful except that we passed an overturned ship's lifeboat which appeared to have been in the sea for some time and we reported but could do nothing about. We reached the Straits of Dover in daylight in bright sunshine which, since our capacity for manoeuvre was extremely limited, we were pleased about as shipping were able to sight us early and keep well clear.

The weather situation quickly deteriorated about noon that day and for the next two days as we headed down the English Channel in beautiful sunshine, we were faced with a series of full gales the unusual weather situation being, according to the forecasters, a "tight pressure gradient".

However, shortly after rounding Ushant and heading SSW to keep south of the on-coming Gulf Stream which would have slowed us down enormously, the weather improved and was to remain so for the rest of the voyage across the "Milk Pond". This was particularly welcome for myself as the automatic winch which paid out and recovered towing wire whenever the pressure of the tow exceeded or fell below twenty tons was going constantly. As a lowly 2nd RO, my cabin was only about ten meters from the winch and its constant rumbling to which I had not yet become used made sleep difficult.

Once into the open ocean we deployed a mile and a half of wire which hung down in a giant bight into the ocean and the winch seldom had to pay out or recover since the tug was no longer "pulling" the mid-section but just straightening the wire and allowing the tow to run up to it. Progress in good weather was about five knots (5.75 mph). The sea water temperature was taken each hour at the engine room cooling water inlet and if it increased by a few degrees, it meant that we were steaming into the Gulf Stream so course had to be altered a few degrees to the south until the temperature dropped again.

This was my first experience of ocean towing and it was a pleasant one. Weather and seas were good and there was little to do other than to stand one six and one two hour watch each day in the radio room. About the only radio traffic was the six hourly weather report to Portishead Radio and the nightly 'sked' with the other tugs in the fleet that were at sea: the fleet consisted of the Overseas Towage and Salvage Company vessels and the Dutch Smith Lloyd vessels.

During this sked, positions and news were exchanged and a brotherly eye was kept on one another. (I had my own private sked with my brother who was an RO on a Greek tanker called the "Zenatia"). I took the midnight to 0600 watch as I loved night-time when radio reception was at its absolute best. Something which was very new to me and which I found thoroughly interesting was to find the European broadcast stations especially the BBC Light Programme and BBC Home Service slowly fading away as we moved west to be gradually replaced by the Newfoundland, Canadian and US radio stations.

For the rest of the crew, life was almost leisurely except for the engine room gang and the ABs on the wheel on the bridge. True, there was the constant life of the chipping hammer and the paint brush, and the splicing of ropes and wires seemed to go on a lot, but most of the day was governed by breakfast, lunch and dinner times and the ringing of the ship's bell to announce the change of watches. Occasionally other vessels were sighted but we were sailing well off the normal shipping lanes, so this was not something that happened frequently.

About halfway across we began to make frequent sightings of Portuguese Men of War jellyfish, their sail fins sticking up proud of the sea's surface and propelling them in the direction of Europe, then flying fish began to appear, skimming from wave crest to wave crest, and then giant swathes of sargassum weed became frequent. We sometimes captured the sargassum in buckets and examined the undersides of the weed with great interest since it was literally alive with crabs, tiny fish, and other items of sea life that we were unable to identify.

Occasionally a loggerhead turtle was sighted as it fed on the jellyfish, and once or twice we caught sight of an albatross as it skimmed effortlessly wave to wave. They always seemed to be curious about our strange procession and came close to have a look. At one time, to great anticipations and excitement, a paravane was made and streamed off the beam in the hope of catching some fresh fish. The paravane worked beautifully but, to our great disappointment, the fishing hooks did not and all they caught was sargassum weed.

Eventually after about thirty days the approach to our destination announced itself by the Captain sending a radio message to our agents in Baltimore ordering the dollars needed to pay everyone a 'sub' from the wages which would be paid at the end of the voyage.

Soon after we arrived off the Chesapeake and, having been closely inspected by the "Peter Stuyvesant" coast guard vessel, so called because to seamen the red stripe on her hull resembled the Peter Stuyvesant cigarette pack, took pilots on board and a day later arrived in Baltimore where the harbour tugs took our mid-section and tied it to one side of the wharf while we tied up opposite on the other side of the wharf.

A crane came trundling down the wharf with a skip on the end of its hook and this was used to quickly transfer the six Dutchmen in the running crew from the mid-section to the towing deck of "Turmoil" where there was much slapping of backs and shaking of hands with smiles all round to celebrate the safe end of the voyage.

We spent a few days in Baltimore – boozy days let it be said, fortunately without incident other than one of the crew being picked up for urinating in public. During this time one of the great joys of our stay was the arrival on board of fresh fruit, fresh vegetables, T-bone steaks and – wonder of wonders – fresh shoreside bread. After a day or two we got orders for New York to pick up a WW2 aircraft carrier called the "Chenango" to be towed to Bilbao in Spain for scrapping.

On arrival in New York, we tied up across the wharf from the "Chenango" in the Hoboken Shipyards. One look at her 553-foot length and 114-foot width as she towered over sixty feet above the wharf was enough to start the old hands on "Turmoil" muttering. Instinctively, everyone knew she was going to be trouble. Our bosun, John L., was heard to have words with someone who suggested that "That bitch is likely to kill the f-----g lot of us". (John L. was a quiet spoken man from Skibbereen in County Cork who had three times been torpedoed during the war, leaving great gouges out of his chest and abdomen: his word was law as far as everyone on "Turmoil" – officers and crew – was concerned).

Access to "Chenango" was by means of a gangway to two gigantic doors in the vessel's side which gave on to one of the hanger decks. Only the hanger deck and the engine room were lit with electric arc lamps, the rest of the ship consisting of what must have been thousands of compartments being in total darkness. In no time, most of the "Turmoil's crew set out to "explore" – explore meaning helping ourselves to anything of value that was not welded down.

The really experienced explorers made an initial reconnaissance to identify pieces of machinery which contained bearings which could later be stripped of their valuable "white metal". Over the next couple of days, a lot of white metal together with other items of copper and bronze came on board the tug and was carefully hidden away.

My job was to rig my radio equipment for the running crew in what had been the bridge and set up the navigation lights. This I succeeded in doing, coming close to disaster when I climbed up into what I found out the hard way was the rotten tangle of masts and spars above the fire control and communications towers. It soon became apparent that underneath the grey paint everything was corroded rotten when the lattice I was climbing gave way and fell to the deck far below.

Having gotten everything in order to the satisfaction of Kor Bass, the skipper of the running crew, I did my own share of exploring, which was a weird experience. The pitch-black alley ways and compartments were never silent and there seemed to be a constant echoing of weird clatters, bangs and ghostly moans going on all the time. I came across the ship's dentist surgery complete with dentist chair and all the fittings and the instruments set out on table and work tops as though the dentist and his staff had just paused work for a minute. Not far from it was the flight readiness room with its padded chairs, screens and charts, and even the names of the air crews who must have been on standby chalked on a board just inside the door.

We had to standby for almost a week as there were major problems with the dockyard's efforts to centre "Chenango's two propellers which, had they not been aligned centrally, would have acted as rudders making her extremely difficult to control when under tow. The only incident was when our cabin boy got separated from an exploring group and had to be rescued by search party.

Eventually, the day came and just after noon New York's famous Moran harbour tugs with their distinctive black funnels marked with the white letter M pulled "Chenango" from the wharf out into the Hudson where they wrestled in increasing numbers with her for two or three hours, causing chaos among the harbour traffic to the extent that coastguard helicopter and a few news helicopters arrived to see what was going on. "Chenango" was not setting out on her last voyage without a struggle, and in a stiff breeze refused to respond to the efforts of the tugs to straighten her up and hand her over to "Turmoil".

On board "Turmoil" everyone watched mostly silently and with enormous misgivings as it seemed our predictions about our tow were proving true even before we left harbour. Eventually, being rigged to the "Chenango" but forbidden to start towing, someone passed the word that we could make a start and, to thunder from the engine room we used every ounce of our 32 tons bollard pull to forcibly drag the "Chenango" from what was rapidly becoming a marine circus past the Statue of Liberty out to Sandy Hook and out into the Atlantic and immediately in foul weather which lasted almost the entire crossing.

Our misgivings about "Chenango" proved themselves all too accurate and, whether in fact someone had made a mess of centering her screws, the tow proved to be extremely difficult to manage in any sort of seaway. At one stage, in really foul weather she decided for three days she was going back to New York and simply dragged us, with everything battened down and seas streaming across decks and past dogged down portholes, backwards and sideways all over the ocean. Most of the time she lay a mile just aft of our beam and at night we had to keep the radar running and keep a sharp look out to make sure she did not come charging out of the darkness and rain to ram us.

By this time, she was an object of hatred to everyone on board the "Turmoil", who thought of her not as a ship but as a thoroughly malign spirit bent on destroying "Turmoil". Eventually we arrived at the Spanish coast just north of Coruna, much further south than we had intended, and began the nerve-racking passage along the cliff and rock strewn north coast of Spain where bad weather from the Bay of Biscay would surely have driven us ashore.

Fortunately, the weather turned good, and we arrived in Bilbao without incident except for the usual harbour tug circus in which the harbour master eventually had to intervene and ask us to remake our link to the bridle of the tow and wrestle her into the dockyard.

A few days later, the Chief Officer took over command from the Captain who, together with the Chief RO, was returning to UK on leave, and three of the crew having been sent home following some unpleasantness ashore, we sailed for Cadiz to pick up another mid-section. Since we would be contract towing, I made the mistake of saying I would be happy to sail alone as the only RO on board and this would turn out to be a small problem later.

We had to wait some weeks for the mid-section to be ready, during which we did make one unsuccessful dash to try to pick up a casualty in the Straits of Gibraltar and ended up spending a few days in Gibraltar itself to do some minor repairs and take on board food and bunkers. In appreciation of the food order, the Chief Steward was presented with three gross of condoms which seemed a bit excessive for a crew of thirty-six men.

During our stay four of us officers crossed the airport runway into Spain to see a bullfight in Algeciras: we were encouraged to leave the bullfight having shouted Ole during the last fight of the night when the bull got the matador. We ended up in a waterfront dive drinking gin which was probably being brewed in a bathtub out the back at the time we were drinking it at the bar. The following day none of us were hardly able to stand, and worries that we were about to go blind abounded.

Returning to Cadiz, we picked up the mid-section and looked forward to a leisurely crossing which we thought would be easier than usual partly because we were now well south in the North Atlantic and also the mid-section had been fitted with a rudimentary 'spoon' bow which should have made it much easier to tow. We were wrong of course because about a week out lunch was interrupted by the ringing of the phone in the dining saloon for the Chief Engineer and the announcement that the scavenge pump on the port side engine had packed in, cutting our speed to well below half which at that time in good weather had been about five knots.

It looked like it could be a long time before we reached the Chesapeake.

It was suggested that we would make for Funchal in Madeira for repairs but following a flurry of radio messages it was decided that spares for the pump would be flown to Cork from Leith and shipped out to us on Smith Lloyd's "Wittesee", which was on station in Cobh at that time. Meantime we continued on, making very poor headway for about ten days even though the weather was quite good.

Eventually the "Wittesee" arrived and the very delicate task of transferring twenty or more enormously heavy packages containing the spares began. The delicacy of the task arose because the transfer had to be by the "Wittesee"'s lifeboat which, because of the very wide running strake around the "Turmoil"'s hull meant that there was a very real prospect that, if the boat's crew got timing was wrong and ran alongside at the wrong moment, she could be trapped under the strake and tipped over.

What appeared from the "Turmoil"'s deck to be a light sea swell running at the time quickly became apparent as a considerable swell, and the possibility of trapping the lifeboat and tipping it over was very real.

In the event, the two tallest men on the ship, Pat Leech, who is in part responsible for this piece of writing, and myself stood wedged in the hawseholes on the towing deck held onto by some of the crew by our belts as we stretched as far out as we could from the "Turmoil"'s towing deck and grabbed hold of the packages as the lifeboat came alongside for a moment.

The transfer took about half an hour and, as some of the packages were really heavy and cumbersome, they left Pat and me with major back pain for days afterwards. With much blowing of sirens, the transfer job having eventually been completed without mishap, the two tugs parted, "Wittesee" for Cobh and "Turmoil" for Baltimore. Repairs on the scavenge pump began immediately and were completed after a couple of days. We then increased speed gradually over the next week to "run in" the repaired pump and eventually reached full speed of a magnificent five knots again. Not for long, though, because two days later a bang was heard from the engine room and the same scavenge pump ended up in pieces on the deck.

Thoroughly fed up with the whole business, a transfer of the tow to another one of Smith Lloyd's tugs was refused and it was decided that we would continue on one engine and take a chance on the good weather holding for what would obviously be a long voyage.

In fact, the weather, which remained reasonably good, proved to be the least of our worries as, after about seventy days, we began to run out of food and fresh water: what things must have been like for our running crew on the mid-section didn't bear thinking about.

Towards the end, on "Turmoil" we were reduced to spam which somehow had survived since WW2 and something called curried rabbit. In the engine room some sort of device was rigged around the condenser to distil fresh water from sea water. "Makey-mendie" was a frequent occupation as our clothes were suffering from constant wear due to the motion of the tug and needed the attention of needle and thread. Some of us had to stop brushing our teeth because our gums would start bleeding, and this was difficult to stop. Halitosis became the order of the day.

As we approached the American coast the weather closed in and we were without noon or star sights for four or five days which meant we were never sure of our exact position. All we knew was that we were not far from land as we could smell the distinctive odour of warm swamp land even though we estimated we were about forty miles off. We knew we were in the Gulf Stream which was running hard in a northerly direction but exactly where we were not sure and this was a cause for considerable worry because being on one engine with limited pulling power, if we became embayed south of the entry to the Chesapeake, we could be in real trouble with a real prospect of running ashore.

Radio was of little use since in that part of the world radio direction finding was extremely unreliable and, because of the low-lying nature of the Virginia and Louisiana topography, at forty miles off radar was of little use. Just as coming about and heading back offshore until the weather cleared, the weather did clear, and a noon day sight confirmed that we were within a few miles of the position which our Second Mate and Master Navigator had plotted.

Later that evening as dusk fell, we picked up two pilots and an inspection team from the US Coast Guard who, having looked at us and the condition we were in departed after giving us permission to proceed one of them being heard to say, "C----t, this is the British navy I had read about but I thought it had gone out with Nelson."

The rest of the voyage was something of an anti-climax as, being only partly under command having had to shorten the tow, making steering a bit hit and miss, we hit a number of navigation buoys on the way up Chesapeake Bay, and we eventually arrived alongside the wharf in the dockyard. The first order of business was one about which we were taking no prisoners; the recovery of our running crew which was accomplished in the usual crane and bucket fashion, but was unusual in that everyone rushed the towing deck to embrace the Dutchmen as they climbed out of the bucket.

The next few days proved to be a bit hazy for everyone, but they did result in a lot of very sore heads, a few arrests and a number of deliveries back to the ship of semi-conscious seamen by police car. No charges were ever made since by this time we had become something of local heroes as the story of our voyage got about. We were told by a policeman that we were all easily identified by the fact that as we walked and staggered along the street it was easy to distinguish between local drunks and seamen who were still having problems finding their land legs.

After a week in which repairs were carried out in the engine room, the usual disillusion with shoreside life began to set in and we were beginning to think about getting back to sea again. The problem was that rumour was rife that we were about to be sent to Norfolk, Virginia, to pick up another aircraft carrier for Spain, and this we certainly did not want to do especially as the weather forecasts which I was monitoring from Portishead were showing the North Atlantic building up into a vicious Winter weather battleground.

In the event, it was finally decided somewhere that the towing season was over for that year and we headed back across light ship, swinging north along the Newfoundland coast up into the southern Denmark Strait past Iceland in search of possible casualties and possible prize money in what was really appalling weather. Two weeks later we raised the Texel Light vessel off the Dutch coast and later that evening tied up in Rotterdam where a day or so later the ship's company paid off and "Turmoil" remained with just a watchman on board for the time being.

I paid off on 22 November 1962 and travelled back on the ferry from Hook of Holland to Harwich and then by train to London and onwards to Fishguard and by overnight ferry to Cork. This ferry trip proved to be the most miserable voyage I had ever experienced up to then as I could not adjust to the motion of the large ship after so long on tiny "Turmoil" and I was seasick all the way.

I had every intention of re-joining "Turmoil" for her next voyage as I had fallen in love with life on salvage tugs, but this was not to be. Instead I was posted to another tug, the "Marinia", which was engaged in contract towing around the British coast which proved tame fare indeed and I soon got fed up and paid off on my birthday 8th May 1963 to join a Greek tanker called the "Virginia" carrying grain from Canada to Novorossiysk on the Russian Black Sea, her Radio Officer having 'lost it' during the voyage and having to be taken off the ship in a straitjacket when the ship berthed in Ceuta, North Africa.

But that is another story.

This short story tells of another side of the rough, tough deep sea tugmen; it was sent to me by Jeannette Tighe in 2017:

> We had the pleasure of visiting Cobh a few weeks ago just before the hurricane and met a lovely gentleman who lives there, who was a crew member on the *Turmoil*. He showed us a picture of the tug and crewmen that hung on the wall of the pub. His name was Buddy Stoat. I was touched by his *Turmoil* stories, his experience as a seaman including riding out the last hurricane at sea and his warmth and friendliness to two American visitors.

The following is from Pat Leech, who had put Sean Cowman (whose fine tale is shown above), in touch with me.

> I was a deckhand on the *Turmoil* until her last trip; we paid off in Pembroke docks, many good times.
>
> Regards
>
> Pat Leech

David Heyes

My brother in law Courtney Jane, served on *Turmoil* out of Falmouth in the 1950s sadly he has just passed away.

Victoria Stanley

My Granddad, Courtney Jane sailed on this ship, always told me about trying to save the enterprise. He passed away on the 29/12/2013.

Fig 113 *Turmoil* at Tilbury landing stage, date unknown (scanned from a slide by the late Ron Hutchins).

Andy Parker

Hi, my great uncle was the captain at the time of the "flying enterprise" incident, Capt Dan Parker, a nice bloke so my dad informed me. I have clippings of the incident, and there is a book around about the *Turmoil*, and even a Tri-ang model (which I have)

Harry

Nice story about gallant tug – real seagoing tug, which kind of tug already forever gone. Thanks for the story

10: *WARDEN*

Just one month after the launch of *Turmoil*, the last of the tugs was ready for launch as Ship No 338. At her launching on 28 June 1945 she would be named HMRT *Warden* by Mrs Diana Falconer.

She was towed around to the fitting-out basin; the war in Europe was over, with the Germans having unconditionally surrendered on the 8th of that month. So, it was to great relief of the attending crowd that she at least would be unlikely to go into action, as most of her six sisters had, as she would probably not be finished before the Japanese would be likely to surrender, ending World War II.

After her fitting out and completion of successful sea trials HMRT *Warden* was commissioned into the Royal Navy in December 1945. She would sail under pennant numbers W170 / A309.

Her start in life did not get off too well with the unfortunate death of her chief cook, Henry Charles Clarke, who was discharged dead while she was still at Leith fitting out. He was buried at Seafield Cemetery just along the road from the Henry Robb Shipyard.

With the end of the war *Warden* was now deemed as surplus to the requirements of the Royal Navy, and she was to be chartered out. She would go on a five-year charter to Risdon A. Beazley Ltd of Southampton, who took her over in December 1946. They promptly

Fig 114 *Warden* (image from RFANostalgia).

Fig 115 *Warden* in Malta.
Photo from RFAA Plymouth.

renamed her *Twyford*, and she would operate as a deep sea salvage tug for the next five years.

Just before her charter, however, another unfortunate death would be recorded on board; on 5 September 1946 greaser Willian John McAdam was discharged dead; he was buried at the Bellshill Cemetery near Glasgow.

The next notable event in the ship's history was recorded when on 15 March 1947 she sailed from Falmouth, proceeding to the aid of *Ernie Pyle*, an American steamer that had broken down off the Isles of Scilly. The steamer recovered power, however, before *Twyford* arrived, so she was unsuccessful in this particular salvage trip.

She continued as a civilian salvage tug until returning to the Admiralty in 1951 and her name reverted to HMS *Warden*. In August 1953 Lieutenant Commander Frederick C. Hard, RN, was appointed in command.

HMS *Warden* sailed out of Cape Town, South Africa, on 26 March 1954 with HMS *Kempenfelt* in tow, heading back to the UK for a refit.

Then the following year, on 6 February four sailors on *Warden* were injured when a towline parted while she was towing the depot ship HMS *Montclare*. A doctor transferred from HMS *Montclare* to give medical aid on *Warden*. All the sailors were taken by lifeboat to St Mary's Hospital on the Isles of Scilly, one of them detained with a more serious injury. The ship had her fair share of injuries and some would say bad luck, as the next year the Suez Crisis would hit the headlines. (For more on the Suez Crisis see Chapter 3.)

October 1956 would see *Warden* take part in Operation Musketeer as she towed a heavy lift crane from Portsmouth to Port Said; she then towed landing craft from Cyprus to Port Said, to put troops ashore.

In 1959 she was transferred to the Royal Fleet Auxiliary and renamed RFA *Warden*.

Perhaps the change of name was lucky for *Warden*, as she would share in a large salvage bounty on 23 September 1960, when members of her crew at this time, along with those of RFA *Sea Salvor*, RFA *Cedardale* and several Royal Navy units, all shared £100,000 salvage money, an exceptionally large sum in 1960. This was for the salvage of two large tankers that had caught fire in the Arabian Sea.

Fig 116 *Warden* in dry dock in Malta. Photo from RFAA Plymouth.

In July 1961 she had a new master, Captain F.R. Murray, RFA. She continued with her towing and salvage duties with the RFA, and then in October 1961 she was towing HMS *Barmouth* in heavy weather in the North Sea when her tow parted, not once but three times in rough seas.

Then again, while towing the frigate HMS *Pheasant* off the north Cornish coast in the stormy month of January 1963, the tow parted twice. The frigate was perhaps reluctant to get to her destination at Troon, Scotland, where she was to be broken up.

In January 1965 the Admiralty decided to place RFA *Warden* in reserve; she was towed to Pembroke Dock by RFA *Typhoon*, another relatively new tug built at Leith. *Warden* would languish in reserve at Pembroke Dock, eventually being offered for sale; she, like *Turmoil*, was purchased by Tsavliris (Salvage & Towage) Ltd, Piraeus, and renamed *Nisos Delos* in September 1969.

She was then sold to Nicolas E. Vernicos Shipping Co. Ltd, Piraeus, and renamed *Vernicos Dimitrios* in 1972.

HMS *Warden*: a short story from Graham Whatmore

I was never one for collecting pictures of my time in the Royal Navy, and I now regret it of course and the few that I had "mysteriously disappeared" after my divorce though I do have a book of the last commission of HMS *Newfoundland* out in the far east from '58 until we brought her home in '59, she was sold to the Peruvian Navy after that commission, a sad end for a great ship.

My memories of life on *Warden* are very vague now of course after all this time but I do remember it being one of the best times in my career, she being such a small ship with a small crew of about 35 including the Captain, a Lt Cdr, a Lt Cdr as Jimmy plus two subbies, one an Australian the other a New Zealander; we knew each other inside out so it was a very friendly crew. As the signalman onboard my duties weren't exactly onerous, so I volunteered for duty on the wheel as part of my watch, something I had always wanted to do, I became in a short time one the skipper's reliable wheelmen and I loved every minute of it. The wheel of course was on the open bridge, ideal for steaming backwards and forwards across the Indian Ocean, and I, like the others, would sit on the high seat steering with my feet, and surprisingly the officer of the watch never corrected us except if we zig zagged a bit.

The Skipper was the most experienced tug master in the RN and an amazing ship handler, it seemed there was nothing that man couldn't do. On the way to Malta from Pompey [Portsmouth] we picked up a tow in Gibraltar, a harbour tug with no power, and four of our crew manning her. We almost immediately went headlong into a storm force gale and in the middle watches the tow broke leaving the harbour tug at the mercy of the storm with no power for steering and we just drifted with her until daylight.

That was one night to remember, and the danger of the tow capsizing was very great of course, but thankfully she got through it and the skipper miraculously managed to pick up the tow by manoeuvring our stern so close to the bow of the tug it was frightening, it was overhanging our stern at times. They had no power, as I said, and four men were unable to take the weight of a six-inch manila which meant we couldn't float it to them, so we had to pass it over their bow which we did eventually and the tow was safe again. All this took place in mountainous seas so it was a magnificent piece of seamanship by our skipper.

To say he was a character would be an understatement, he loved his gin and often came on the bridge in a state of, shall we say, "happy" and I well remember his habit of bringing a revolver as well to shoot cowboy style at the flying fish. The officer of the watch used to clear the foc'sle when he did this because his aim wasn't very good to say the least and made worse by the bottle of gin inside him. Ha, ha, ha! Happy days.

After our last tow we stopped in Aden as usual and the skipper sold all the tow ropes, (seriously,) as they would not be needed any more. He bought us a couple of barrels of beer on the proceeds and we sat on the tow deck most of the night until we finished them off. The poor 1st Lieutenant was an ex public schoolboy, very posh and exactly the opposite to the skipper who was a very down to earth hard bitten tug master, and the skipper didn't like him one bit, it must have been a bad period of his life I think.

Fig 117 RFA *Warden* in her prime: under way, all shipshape and Bristol fashion (image owner unknown).

We all quickly learned to keep out of his way in the mornings, he always had a hangover and was not very sociable until the steward fetched him his daily dose of gin after which he was one of the lads again. The two subbies must have been amazed at the casualness of life onboard and lack of discipline, but they knew better than try to impose it, it was unnecessary because everyone did their job regardless and even our tot was always neaters, which was totally against Navy rules and regs, to be honest I do not think the skipper would have allowed it anyway.

I believe she was de-commissioned on our return to the UK and taken over by the RFA but I may be mistaken in that assumption, it was a long time ago. She was a happy ship with a happy crew, but so unlike the usual naval vessel as to be almost civvy in its running, but no one can ever doubt how efficient she was.

Warden was eventually broken up in Perama in October 1992, her near-50 years a degree of longevity for any ship and another fine testament to her builders and to all the tugmen who served on her.

Terence Charles Cole

I served on the *Warden* as a Leading Steward from 1957 to1959. One job the tug carried out was to tow SS *Melika* from Muscat to Scilly, for which we received Salvage money. I spent my happiest years in the RN on her.

Graham Whatmore

I served on Warden in 1960. We towed coastal minesweepers two at a time from Malta to Singapore via the Suez Canal. We had two trips then returned

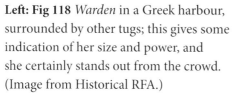

Left: Fig 118 *Warden* in a Greek harbour, surrounded by other tugs; this gives some indication of her size and power, and she certainly stands out from the crowd. (Image from Historical RFA.)

Right: Fig 119 As *Vernicos Dimitrios*, looking rather rusty in Greece (image from Historical RFA).

to Pompey where I was drafted back to HMS *Mercury*, I was a Signalman. It seemed strange as a rating to have a cabin between two of us, my cabin mate was the sparker. Great few months they were and I didn't want it to end, but she was to be de-commissioned so that was it.

I leave the last words in this book to the recollections of Ernest Cooper:

Some recollections of an apprentice in Henry Robb Shipyard during World War II

Ernest Cooper, MBE CE FiMechE (85 at the time of writing)

Served apprenticeship 1941–45 in Robb's sandwich [course], Heriot Watt, corvettes, Bustler tugs etc.

A start in life never to be forgotten, and in today's world no longer possible.

I was transferred from the machine shop to the yard. The demands of the war had exceeded the availability of male workers. Women in large numbers were recruited to be 'chippers and painters' in the yard. They were the toughest breed you could imagine. Woe betides an apprentice caught alone in an area where they were working. He would be very fortunate if he managed to escape being their plaything and just to lose his pants. One unfortunate was kept captive for a day and emerged a shattered wreck. It was so bad that the apprentices went on strike and demanded protection, which was given by the management.

I was learning about the other side of life.

Apprentices were a skiving lot. We would avoid work at every opportunity, and I was no exception.

My recollection of the most outstanding ship that I worked on was the Bustler class tugs. These were naval vessels designed to pull a 10,000-ton ship at 10 knots. They had yacht-like lines and had two Polar Atlas diesel engines driving one propeller through a Vulcan gearbox developing 10,000 HP. The accommodation was of very high order specially adapted to deal with survivors.

When they were launched, we all had a gut feeling that they would be special.

11: TECHNICAL SPECIFICATIONS OF THE TUGS AS BUILT

During the 1930s, while Great Britain was a world superpower still with most of its empire in place, along with the world's largest navy, there was one area where the British fell behind: the lack of ocean-going tugs. The Dutch had the really large, powerful tugs at the time, and to compete with them Henry Robb designed some powerful ocean-going tugs for overseas owners (see Chapter 2).

Robb had designed a large powerful twin-engine tug just before the start of World War II for Overseas Towage and Salvage Ltd. Some of the large ocean-going tugs designed before had been twin-screw, but as mentioned in Chapter 2, the latest of these, *Abeille No 8*, for French owners, launched in 1936, had been given twin engines coupled to a single propeller.

When the Admiralty were looking around at large tugs for use during World War II the thinking was still around steam-powered tugs, but Robb managed to persuade them to consider twin-engine diesels coupled to a single propeller. This arrangement proved to be considerably more powerful than the largest Dutch tug, *Zwarte Zee*; while she had a bollard pull of 24 tons, *Bustler* was rated at no less than 30.

The following specifications and information were originally shown on my earlier website, Leith Shipyards. (My current site is www.theloftsman.com.) The information came from the original shipyard build books which record the details of each ship built.

HMRT *BUSTLER*, SHIP NO 321

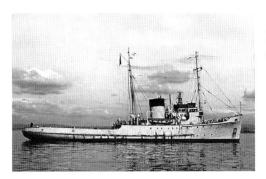

Fig 120 HMRT *Bustler*, the lead Bustler class rescue tug (image, Historical RFA).

Owners	Royal Navy		
Registered		**Keel laid**	01/02/1941
Type of ship	Ocean rescue/salvage tug	**Launched**	04/12/1941
		Commissioned	14/05/1942
Ship details			
Length overall	205' 0"	**Launch details**	
Length B.P.	190' 0"	**Weather**	
Beam	38' 6"	**Time to water**	
Depth Mld	19' 0"		
Draught	6' 11"		
GRT	1,100 tons		
DWT			
Complement	42 officers and men		
Engines	2 × 8-cylinder diesels (Atlas Polar), bhp 3,020		
Props	1		
Speed	16 knots		
Armament	1 × 12-pdr AA gun, 1 × 2-pdr AA, 2 × 20mm AA and 4 × Lewis .303 machine guns		
Other known names	1973 *Mocni*, 1975 *Smjeli*		
Current status	Broken up in Yugoslavia 1989		

HMRT *SAMSON*, SHIP NO 322

Fig 121 HMRT *Samsonia* (ex-*Samson*), the second Bustler class rescue tug, with her RFA number, A 218 (image, Historical RFA).

Owners	Royal Navy		
Registered	Admiralty	**Keel laid**	01/02/1942
Type of ship	Ocean rescue/salvage tug	**Launched**	01/04/1942
		Commissioned	14/09/1942
Ship details			
Length overall	205' 0"	**Launch details**	
Length B.P.	190' 0"	**Weather**	
Beam	38' 6"	**Time to water**	
Depth Mld	19' 0"		
Draught	16' 11"		
GRT	1,100 tons		
DWT			
Complement	42 officers and men		
Engines	2 × 8-cylinder diesels (Atlas Polar M48M) bhp 3,020		
Props	1		
Speed	16 knots		
Armament	1 × 12-pdr AA gun, 1 × 2-pdr AA, 2 × 20mm AA and 4 × Lewis .303 machine guns		
Other known names	1942 *Samsonia*, 1947 *Foundation Josephine*, 1974 *Jaki*		
Current status	Broken up 1979		

HMRT *GROWLER*, SHIP NO 328

Fig 122 As RMAS *Cyclone* (image from RfaNostalgia).

Owners	Royal Navy		
Registered		**Keel laid**	31/01/1942
Type of ship	Ocean rescue/salvage tug	**Launched**	10/09/1942
		Commissioned	16/03/1943
Ship details			
Length overall	205' 0"	**Launch details**	
Length B.P.	190' 0"	**Weather**	
Beam	38' 6"	**Time to water**	
Depth Mld	19' 0"		
Draught	16' 11"		
GRT	1,100 tons		
DWT			
Complement	42 officers and men		
Engines	2 × 8-cylinder diesels (Atlas Polar) producing 3,020 bhp		
Props	1		
Speed	16 knots		
Armament	1 × 12-pdr AA gun, 1 × 2-pdr AA, 2 × 20mm AA and 4 × Lewis .303 machine guns		
Other known names	1947 Caroline Moller, 1952 Castle Peak, 1958 Welshman, 1963 Cyclone (pennant A 111), 1983 Martial		
Current status	Broken up in 1985		

HMRT *HESPERIA*, SHIP NO 329

Fig 123 HMS *Bustler*, sister ship of *Hesperia* (image, Historical RFA).

Owners	Royal Navy		
Registered		**Keel laid**	25/03/1942
Type of ship	Ocean rescue/salvage tug	**Launched**	10/10/1942
		Commissioned	21/05/1943
Ship details			
Length overall	205' 0"	**Launch details**	
Length B.P.	190' 0"	**Weather**	
Beam	38' 6"	**Time to water**	
Depth Mld	19' 0"		
Draught	16' 11"		
GRT	1,100 tons		
DWT			
Complement	42 officers and men		
Engines	2 × 8-cylinder diesels (Atlas Polar) producing 3,020 bhp		
Props	1		
Speed	16 knots		
Armament	1 × 12-pdr AA gun, 1 × 2-pdr AA, 2 × 20mm AA, and 4 × Lewis .303 machine guns		
Other known names	N/A		
Current status	Lost during a fierce storm in the Mediterranean off Libya on 9 February 1945		

HMRT *MEDIATOR*, SHIP NO 335

Fig 124 RFA *Mediator* with her canvas bridge cover to offer some protection from the sun. The photograph is a little bit damaged but shows her steaming out of Malta. (Photo credit unknown.)

Owners	Royal Navy			
Registered		**Keel laid**	
Type of ship	Ocean rescue/salvage tug	**Launched**	21/04/1944
		Commissioned	
Ship details			
Length overall	205' 0"	**Launch details**	
Length B.P.	190' 0"	**Weather**	
Beam	38' 6"	**Time to water**	
Depth Mld	19' 0"		
Draught	16' 11"		
GRT	1,100 tons		
DWT			
Complement	42 officers and men		
Engines	2 × 8-cylinder diesels (Atlas Polar) producing 3,020 bhp		
Props	1		
Speed	16 knots		
Armament	1 × 12-pdr AA gun, 1 × 2-pdr AA, 2 × 20mm AA and 4 × Lewis .303 machine guns		
Other known names	1965-*Nisos Zakynthos*		
Current status	Unknown: as *Atlas* after her purchase by Maritime Commercial Enterprises Ltd, she was in service from 1975 until 1985, when she was struck from Lloyd's register.		

Fig 125 HMS *Mediator*, engine room, Lister generator, starboard side.
Main engine, Atlas Polar (photograph sent to me by Clive Reynolds).

HMRT *REWARD*, SHIP NO 336

Fig 126 As RFA *Reward* from 1963 to 1971 (image from RfaNostalgia).

Owners	Royal Navy		
Registered		**Keel laid**	06/04/1944
Type of ship	Ocean rescue/salvage tug	**Launched**	31/10/1944
		Commissioned	
Ship details			
Length overall	205' 0"	**Launch details**	
Length B.P.	190' 0"	**Weather**	
Beam	38' 6"	**Time to water**	
Depth Mld	19' 0"		
Draught	16' 11"		
GRT	1,136 tons		
DWT	1,800 tons		
Complement	42 officers and men		
Engines	2 × 8-cylinder diesels (Atlas Polar) producing 3,020 bhp		
Props	1		
Speed	16 knots		
Armament	1 × 3" AA gun, 1 × 2-pdr pom-pom, 2 × 20mm AA guns		
Other known names	1962 *Englishman*, 1975 HMS *Reward*		
Current status	1976 scrapped		

HMRT *TURMOIL*, SHIP NO 337

Fig 127 *Turmoil* during a rescue in 1951 (image source unknown).

Owners	Royal Navy		
Registered		**Keel laid**	14/07/1944
Type of ship	Ocean rescue/salvage tug	**Launched**	11/05/1945
		Commissioned	14/07/1945
Ship details			
Length overall	205' 0"	**Launch details**	
Length B.P.	190' 0"	**Weather**	
Beam	38' 6"	**Time to water**	
Depth Mld	19' 0"		
Draught	16' 11"		
GRT	1,136 tons		
DWT			
Complement	42 officers and men		
Engines	2 × 8-cylinder diesel engines (Atlas Polar) producing, 4,000 bhp		
Props	1		
Speed	16 knots		
Armament	1 × 3" AA gun, 1 × 2-pdr pom-pom, 2 × 20mm AA guns		
Other known names	1957 RFA *Turmoil*, 1965 *Nisos Kerkyra*, 1971 *Matsas*		
Current status	Broken up in Greece in 1986		

HMRT *WARDEN*, SHIP NO 338

Fig 128 Last but not least: HMRT *Warden* was the final Bustler class tug. (Image from RfaNostalgia.)

Owners	Royal Navy		
Registered		**Keel laid**	
Type of ship	Ocean rescue/salvage tug	**Launched**	28/06/1945
		Commissioned	
Ship details			
Length overall	205' 0"	**Launch details**	
Length B.P.	190' 0"	**Weather**	
Beam	38' 6"	**Time to water**	
Depth Mld	19' 0"		
Draught	16' 11"		
GRT	1136 tons		
DWT			
Complement	42 officers and men		
Engines	2 × Atlas Polar 8-cylinder diesel engines, producing 4,000 bhp		
Props	1		
Speed	16 knots		
Armament	1 × 3" AA gun, 1 × 2-pdr pom-pom, 2 × 20mm AA guns		
Other known names	1946 *Twyford*, 1959 RFA *Warden*, 1969 *Nisos Delos*, 1972 *Vernicos Dimitrios*		
Current status	Broken up in 1992		

SOURCES

I have tried to write this book to shine a light on the men and ships that served for so long during times such as we would hope never to see again in this world. Their story has so often been glossed over and is little known, as these vessels never served as large fast warships, speeding through the seas on the chase for the enemy.

These special ships, manned by special men, were tasked with saving and not destroying. Such was their lot during the long years of World War II that they deserve much more recognition than so far given. I hope this book helps just a little. If you have a love of ships and the sea, then this is your book. The story of the brave men and their small ships built at Leith should never be forgotten, and this book is my way of acknowledging this fact.

The sources used come from a very broad range of information, some of the best information coming direct from the men and women who were there, not just from dry research in dusty old library archives – although through necessity the sources too are becoming very important, as we are slowly losing a lot of our great maritime history. This book, the third in a series of four, is my attempt to keep some of that history alive. The other, mostly larger, ships built during World War II will have a book to themselves covering this time at the Leith shipyards, bringing the history of the ships right up to date.

The comments that were sent into my original website on the Leith shipyards have been saved where possible and used in the category where they were originally placed.

As this book deals with the World War II years, the number of first-hand accounts becomes ever lower. Much use is made of the internet; the data in my own original website was a particularly good source of material, and I have used it extensively throughout the series. Where I have found contradictory sources, I have then used my own judgement as a shipbuilder, along with the shipyard's original build order books – even when some of the early entries are missing or unclear – to draw a conclusion.

The following are just some of the websites that you too may find useful:

www.theloftsman.com

http://www.imo.org

www.historicalrfa.org, along with http://www.rfanostalgia.org/ ; the interest shown by the members was amazing and their help was much appreciated, as was that of the good people at the Royal Fleet Auxiliary Association Plymouth – Serving the RFA Community: Rfaaplymouth.org.

Scottish newspapers

www.archive.scotsman.com; this website will charge you a fee for accessing the records.

Other Edinburgh newspapers are held on microfilm in The Edinburgh Room, Edinburgh Central Library, King George IV Bridge, Edinburgh, EH1 1 EG: Edinburgh.room@ edinburgh.gov.uk .

Glasgow newspapers are held by The Mitchell Library, North Street, Glasgow, G3 7DN, archives@cls.glasgow.gov.uk .

I have found that the museums and State Libraries of Australia have been a very helpful resource for information, including those in Adelaide, Victoria, New South Wales and Brisbane.

Museums in New Zealand, too, were once more extremely helpful and a good source of information.

Of course, we should not discount Wikipedia, it just takes a little bit longer, as one does need to check the information shown, as it is not always correct – but as a starting point, and at no cost, you will not find better.

If you have the name of the ship, preferably with the year she was built, type it into any of the internet search engines and you should be able to find some information.

BIBLIOGRAPHY

If you are interested in a particularly good read about the life and work of the deep sea rescue tug *Turmoil*, Ewart Brooks wrote the book *Turmoil* back in 1956; it is a terrific read and a real insight into tug life, both salvaging and towing.

I also recommend *The Grey Seas Under* by Farley Mowat about the perilous rescue missions of a North Atlantic salvage tug.

I have also mentioned *The Tattie Lads* in this book.

Also, see my other books on the ships built at Leith, available from Whittles Publishing and good book shops.

ACKNOWLEDGEMENTS

This series of books would not have been possible without the help of many people, some sadly no longer with us; if anyone is missed this is only down to my own forgetfulness, and I apologise in advance. There are just too many to fit in here, but you know who you are and you have my thanks.

Special mention to Robert Rowbottom and John Knubley who supplied me with information for this book.

To all the men of the Leith Shipyard who influenced me in one way or another.

Ernest Cooper for the use of some of his amazing memoirs; to the many people who have contributions in the book and who are are acknowledged with their story. I have also included many of the comments that were sent into my old website; this book is also about the men and women who served or sailed on a Leith-built ship.

Please note that some of the information shown on the Bustler class rescue tugs is provided by HistoricalRFA who very kindly allowed me access to the archive they hold on the internet.

Some information has been kindly provided by rfaPlymouth as well, and my thanks go to the guys for keeping this history going.

To Barry & Shaun from rfanostalgia, for more time and help than I ever expected. Many thanks go to these guys, along with the other RFA associations who provided images and information.

Also to Chris White of the www.historicalrfa.org website.

To the indomitable John Hargreaves, who kindly provided his story about the secret tow of HMS *Seraph*.

To Dr Keith Whittles and his team for believing in my project, and allowing me to bring this series of books to a wider public.

To Caroline Petherick at https://www.the-wordsmith.co.uk, for providing great direction and guidance in the completion of my book; she has been a pleasure to work with.

To my darling wife Angie, who has the patience of a saint, always believing in me and encouraging me to reach for my dreams, to persevere and to never give up.